GO F

GO FREE

A Guide to Aligning with the Archetype of Westernkind

Creator and author Jason Köhne

With collaboration from others

First Edition 2017

Second Edition 2019

Second Edition Iteration II 2021

Jason Köhne is also the author of *Born Guilty—Liable for Compensation Subject to Retaliation*, *Prometheus Rising—Take Back Your Destiny*, *Crucible—Child Patriot American Victory*, and *It's a Comedy Dammit!*.

Jason Köhne (/ˈkuːnə/ *koo-nuh*)

Printed by CreateSpace

NUG
Productions

Dedication

I dedicate this work to white children. They will suffer far more than we have if we do not secure the well-being of Westernkind.

Important Note: Friends, as I am a vocal champion for White Wellbeing, the antiwhites relentlessly endeavor to ruin me. I am not immune to these attacks. I need your help to stay afloat. Are you able to provide legal, financial, or some other assistance? Please reach out to me:

Hubs: NoWhiteGuilt.org & TheAfterParty.tv
Collectibles: NoWhiteGuiltCollectibles.com
Links: NoWhiteGuilt.org/Links

Thank you.

A Message to All Races, Peoples, and Groups

The primary focus of this book is on countering the harm that antiwhitism inflicts on Westernkind; therefore, the reader is often addressed as a white person. Nevertheless, people of all races are invited to read this book and to learn about the evil of antiwhitism, how to identify it, and how to oppose it.

I invite everyone—of every race, religion, and group—to join us in our efforts to put a stop to antiwhitism. Antiwhitism is at the root of everything destroying all that we have come to cherish and need as freedom loving men and women in Western Civilization.

Please join us in our service to White Wellbeing to put an end to the persecution of Westernkind, particularly the most vulnerable members of the white race: our children, our elderly, our poor, and our sick. I speak for all Westmen in service to White Wellbeing when I say that we proudly honor all nonwhite people who have already added their voices to ours; in an age when you could turn a blind eye on us and enjoy the spoils of antiwhitism, you have shown yourselves to be among the best of humanity. God bless you.

Contents

Notate Bene

To Attain the Benefits of Going Free

To **Go Free**, you must approach this volume with maturity. You must thoughtfully consider the arguments and participate in the interactive segments.

This work is for people who are genuinely interested in aligning with the archetype, committed to accessing the foundations for perfect health, and reaching one's full mental, physical, and spiritual potential as a member of **Westernkind**.

On Vocabulary

I have coined and adopted novel words and phrases to facilitate the process of Going Free by breaking away from the terminology, and hence the thought patterns, of the **antiwhite Regime**. These terms are underlined and highlighted in bold when they first appear, indicating that there is an associated glossary entry in the appendices to this book. Please refer to the glossary when you require clarification.

I wish to stress and reiterate that these novel words and phrases are not mere aesthetic choices, but tools to carefully set a frame for conscious and, importantly, *subconscious* thought so as to effectively bypass (as well as to expose) ingrained antiwhite thought patterns. Sometimes vocabulary is introduced to give names to new, useful concepts; other times it is introduced as a more effective substitute for existing terminology that has been (or always had been) corrupted by antiwhite or otherwise self-defeating associations. The vocabulary used in this book is also carefully chosen to be most resilient against antiwhite corruption in the future.

I recommend that you learn and use the vocabulary presented. However, it is inevitable that some people will be reluctant to use novel terms, and to these people I ask that they at least consider and take on board *the lesson* underlying each new word or phrase, as each is presented for a purpose.

On the Word "White"

I use the word "white" because it is globally used to represent Europeans and European-derived peoples, but I prefer my own terms: **Westman**, **Westmen**, and **Westernkind**. In brief, "white" falls short of conveying peoplehood; however, Westman, Westmen, and Westernkind encapsulate the rich depth and beautiful variety of our people. We often say that *we are a single people with many countries*. These terms are also instantly recognizable to most people, even though they never encountered them before.

"White" is also used to delegitimize and even deny that Westernkind exists. Antiwhites speciously argue that the only difference among the races of man is skin color, and that the "white race" does not exist because it lacks a single set of cultural markers. Westernkind has developed many hues of **Western** culture, and by using Westman, Westmen, and Westernkind, we empower ourselves and invalidate many antiwhite arguments.

On the Word "Antiwhitism"

In the **white sympathetic sphere** of the early '90s, the thought leaders would variously identify a multitude of ideologies and ideologues as the primary drivers of the social ills damaging our communities. I perceived that the constant thread between them was that they victimized *us* primarily, and that was when the idea hit me. We were white, and our victimizers were *antiwhite*.

But *antiwhite* wasn't in my dictionary, nor the dictionaries at the city library.

I was disappointed that such a straightforward and powerful concept was not legitimized by authoritative sources, but I refused to abandon it—it was too perfect. I began using the term to great effect in all of my advocacy. Within weeks, I had added *-ism* to the end of *antiwhite* to identify the superset **antiwhitism** in which all of the subset ideologies were contained.

Despite being well received by most, **white sympathetic** organizational and thought leaders criticized my use of the terms because they weren't "official."

Decades later, on August 23, 2020, a heroic practitioner of Going Free (thank you FinalBlossom!) shared with me a damning discovery he made in a nearly 50-year-old dictionary:

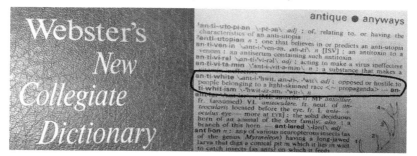

Antiwhite and *antiwhitism* were there.

Through the decades, not only were antiwhites creating and corrupting words to victimize us, they were deleting them too. They had removed *antiwhite* and *antiwhitism* from our vocabulary to deny us the power of these concepts. The reality is that we think in words; *if we do not have the words for our defense, we cannot think or act in our own defense.* Let this manipulation of the dictionary be your first proof of the power of words, and in the power of having a lexicon tailored to serve your need, as this book seeks to provide.

To have finally gained the added legitimacy of an official endorsement was very welcome, but there is another lesson here: Just because something is not in the dictionary, or is not currently in popular use, does not mean that it is not valuable to you—sometimes it is absent precisely because it is!

In the words of Cicero and the vow of Hamlet:

The safety of the people shall be the highest law.

I will speak daggers but use none.

Level One:

External Threats

Welcome to the

1ˢᵗ Level of Going Free

Congratulations on making one of the best decisions of your life! Over many years of experimentation, thousands of dollars, and untold hours in research and interviewing, I have developed the **Archetype Alignment Protocol (AAP)**—the practice you will use to align yourself with the archetype of **Westernkind**—the practice you will use to **Go Free**. Going Free is the only path to purifying yourself of the deep-seated toxic beliefs undermining your life.

By way of this work, you will come to understand the disease inflicted upon us, a disease I call **white-noir**. You will be given the tools to cure yourself by identifying, treating, and immunizing yourself against **meme-pathogens (MPs)** that cause white-noir. As you Go Free, you will awaken the ancient and suppressed potential of Westernkind within you. You will thereby increase your **potential-to-power (PTP)**.

You will be counted among a rapidly growing community of our best people, **Westmen** who are discovering improvements in their abilities by dedicating themselves to the AAP.

Going Free on a global scale will restore tranquility, order, and safety to Western Civilization by restoring bodily, emotional, and spiritual harmony to Westernkind. Your decision to Go Free will not only break your own chains, but it will break the chains on our people.

How I Came to Be with You

I was born and raised in the Washington, D.C. area and discovered **antiwhitism** as a child. **Antiwhite** verbal abuse and street fights with antiwhite thugs shaped and steeled me. While still a youth, I dedicated my life to freeing Westmen from antiwhitism, thereby unlocking their full potential.

I was a star athlete and graduated university with highest honors. I am an author, maverick, adventurer, and researcher who has spent the equivalent of several lifetimes examining Westernkind's challenges and formulating a path to the recapture of our destiny.

Passionate about my life's quest, yet humbly aware of a man's limitations, I combed through many disciplines, dissecting the most gifted minds and extracting the pearls of their genius. Recognizing my dedication to our people, many venerable researchers and thinkers honored me with private meetings, whereat I gleaned their profound accumulated wisdom.

Combining diverse and widespread schools of thought, I bridged the gap between science and spirituality. The achievement of that lifelong research is the AAP.

This volume is your first step to Going Free. Reading and completing the activities will lead you to a healthier, freer, and more powerful future. You will learn to unlock within yourself the greatest power the world has ever known: Western Man.

An important warning before continuing: Do not look to the **Regime** (the governments, international banks, news and entertainment media, and academia) for permission, validation, or approval to Go Free. These purveyors of antiwhitism and the **Antiwhite Narrative** do not want you to Go Free. Their opposition, as you will come to understand, is proof that you have made the right decision.

Let's begin.

Level One: External Threats

The Level One (L1) material is designed to help you identify external threats. These external threats are the MPs in the world around you. Like other pathogens, MPs infect you and undermine your ability to achieve your goals and satisfy your desires. MPs also undermine our natural inclination to identify with our people, which is necessary to achieve lasting individual well-being.

Developing the L1 skillsets is your first step to Going Free—enabling you to climb higher toward your full mental, physical, and spiritual potential as a **Westman**.

A Boy Named Buddy Smith

Imagine a boy named Buddy Smith, a normal **Western** boy in every way. His mother and father are devoted to him, giving him attention, education, affection, and tenderness. He plays a musical instrument and is involved in sports. He enjoys home-cooked meals every night.

Buddy is always smiling. He throws his arms around his friends for group photos. He climbs into a soft bed every evening, gets a kiss good night, and rests peacefully in a charming house in a safe neighborhood.

But every day a malevolent force haunts young Buddy.

This evil has no face, because it wears many faces. It has no voice, because it speaks with many voices. It tells Buddy that people with his last name are dumb. It backs up this claim with a seemingly endless litany of historical and contemporary stories about Smiths who are dumb. His trusting eyes widen with each one he hears.

This force is active at home and at school. It speaks in the movies and TV shows Buddy watches. It whispers in the books he reads. It is woven into the video games he plays. It stalks at the edges of his friends' conversations. It is even there when his parents speak to him. Buddy's parents do not protect him from this malevolent force because, even if they are aware of it, they fear it and unintentionally reinforce it. The message that Smiths are dumb is everywhere.

So, like everyone else, Buddy becomes a believer. How could it be otherwise? He is just a little boy and the messages come from big people with important positions in his life and in society. No one ever contradicts it. There is no escape. Smiths are dumb.

What is the consequence of a lifetime of days filled with the message *"Smiths are dumb?"* Buddy probably won't try hard to be a success at school, since he knows that people like him are stupid. He may not try to get into college or master a trade. Why bother? He won't explore subjects that interest him because he figures he'll be too dumb to understand them. He'll do nothing to make himself valuable to an employer, or start a healthy family, or provide for his future because these are unattainable dreams for a dumb Smith.

Or perhaps Buddy will swing to the other extreme. He will prove that he is not like the Smiths that came before. He will socially signal that he is different in every way—opposite in every way. He's not dumb like them. Smiths—they are stupid—but *he* is smart. In fact, he is so unlike the other Smiths that he joins the chorus against them. *"Smiths are dumb!"* he shouts. And, in the end, he changes his name and denies he ever was a Smith.

How much more harmful might it have been for young Buddy if, instead of merely being told Smiths were stupid, he was taught that they were *bad*? What if Buddy had been taught that Smiths had always inflicted undeserved suffering on everyone else? What if Buddy had been taught that it wasn't just those who shared his last name, but everyone related to him was evil? What are the costs of these disfiguring beliefs?

Likewise, how might redheaded Tommy be affected by the message that all redheads exploit others? Might he assume exploitative intent in himself even when it is not there? What might this do to his perception of himself and other redheads? Might he even come to identify with the enemies of redheads?

How might Lilly, a young Swede, be affected by the belief that all Swedes are oppressors? Might she become hypersensitive to Swedish cultural expression as tainted by the Swedish desire to oppress? Might the sight of Swedes evoke her disgust? Might she join a movement that militates against Swedes?

How much worse could this have been for Buddy, Tommy, and Lilly if it wasn't their name, hair color, or nationality, but rather the entire extended family of their race? While names, hair color, and nationality can be changed, a person's race is inescapable.

How might this *blood libel*, this identifying as born guilty of "exploitation" and "oppression" undermine their abilities to achieve? How might their beliefs cause them to make disastrous life decisions? How might their beliefs have damaged their characters?

Meme-Pathogens

"Meme" is a term originally coined by scientist Richard Dawkins in his book *The Selfish Gene* (1976). It refers to ideas, beliefs, and behavioral patterns which spread from person to person through a society in a manner analogous to the transmission of genes. Like genes, memes self-replicate, mutate, and are subject to selective pressures.

A *pathogen* is anything that can cause disease. A disease interferes with the proper functionality of a living organism.

A **meme-pathogen (MP)** is a thought or idea that is destructive for the individual or group who holds it. In the practice of Going Free, MPs mostly refer specifically to *antiwhite MPs*: thoughts or ideas that produce physical, mental, emotional, or spiritual disease in Westernkind. They are *lesions* on our bodies, minds, and spirits. For example, any belief that white-guilts or imposes one-sided moral, intellectual, or sentimental obligations on us that weaken our people in any way is an MP.

From the very beginning of our lives, we are infected (indoctrinated) with MPs. Some MPs are superficial, for example *"Westmen can't dance"* and *"Westmen can't jump."* Other MPs attribute psychotic or evil traits to us, such as the following:

- Hateful (either unconsciously or consciously)
- Uniquely wicked
- Morally inferior
- Intellectual thieves
- Predators
- Corrupters
- Persecutors
- Exploiters
- Slave traders

The inescapable harmful conclusions of these MPs:

- *"Westernkind is responsible for the historical lack of achievement and failures of nonwhites."*
- *"Westernkind's accomplishments are products of 'privilege,' undeserved wealth, and the exploitation of nonwhites."*
- *"Nonwhites are 'peoples,' such as Arabic, Asian, and African-American. Westernkind is not a 'people.'"*

- *"Westmen concerned with the well-being of Westernkind are psychotic, dangerous, and genocidal."*
- *"Westmen are intrinsically villainous. Nonwhites are intrinsically virtuous (and are only driven to bad behavior by Westmen)."*

Some specific MPs you are almost certainly infected with:

- *"We all bleed red."*
- *"The white race is uniquely responsible for slavery."*
- *"Institutional racism."*
- *"Diversity is our strength."*
- *"We are a nation of immigrants."*
- *"Structural racism."*
- *"Love is blind."*
- *"White privilege."*
- *"There is no white culture."*
- *"The white race does not exist."*

See Appendices for an expanded list of MPs and **MCs**.

MPs consist of *two parts*: 1. An **antiwhite precept**, which is any notion/idea/thought that slanders, denigrates or otherwise advocates for, or results in, the harming of Westmen. 2. An **interpretive mandate** relative to the precept, i.e. mental conditioning that provokes certain emotions in association with the antiwhite precept.

Thus, the power of MPs is increased by a feedback loop regarding how we are supposed to think and feel about each MP, people who espouse them, and those who disagree.

Consider most of the movies you've seen and how the heroes and villains are portrayed. The characters who work against **White Wellbeing** are intelligent, conscientious, and moral—all admirable qualities we naturally desire to mimic. Conversely, those concerned with White Wellbeing are stupid, cruel, selfish, ugly, and even psychopathic. In every aspect of popular culture, MPs continually influence and misshape our people.

This antiwhite feedback loop permeates all facets of our societies. We are infected with MPs in thousands of ways throughout our lives. This truth may be new to you because often people imagine "indoctrination" as something that is explicit and simple to perceive.

That kind of explicit indoctrination does happen. However, it lacks the power and enduring effects of subtle or insidious infection.

People are naturally suspicious and defensive when they are confronted with overt commandments, punishments, and persuasion attempts. MP infection bypasses these defensive mechanisms with clever delivery systems that I address in the following pages.

Lastly, in casual speech you may also refer to an MP as "an antiwhitism", and reference MPs as "antiwhitisms."

Meme-Pathogen Infection:

Entertainment and

Your Subconscious Mind

The most effective and insidious form of MP infection is entertainment. When being entertained, we lower our defenses—we suspend disbelief and critical judgment. We do not suspect that we are being infected. Thus, we are all the more susceptible. Additionally, in such a context, we are exposing the deepest and richest soil in our psyches to antiwhitism—our subconscious.

First, I want to clarify what I mean by "subconscious mind." I am using the concept as it is popularly understood: thoughts and behavior that are learned and become automatic, but can be altered or counteracted by conscious effort. I am not using the definitions supplied by Friedrich Schelling, Samuel Coleridge, and the discredited Sigmund Freud.

What are the conscious and subconscious minds?

The conscious mind is self-directed. Its highest form is self-reflective. It is slow and cumbersome relative to the subconscious mind. It requires effort, whereas the subconscious does not. Think of the conscious effort invested to learn the location of keys on a keyboard. You had to search for keys and deliberately press them with the proper fingers. That effort interrupted the message you were trying to type.

But once you learned the location of the keys, your subconscious took over the task of typing, and you were able to swiftly type your messages without a single thought to locating the keys.

The subconscious mind is autopilot. It is lightning speed relative to the conscious mind. It is agile relative to the cumbersome conscious. And most important of all, it requires no effort from you.

We are able to override our subconscious with our conscious mind, but doing so requires effort. Recall the effort you consciously invested when breaking a habit—a subconsciously driven thought or behavior.

Did you used to crack your knuckles or take the escalator rather than the stairs without giving a conscious thought to either act? Did you used to order whole rather than skim milk with your coffee? Did you used to lose your temper rather than remain calm when arguing with family or colleagues? Before forcing yourself to take a mature position, did you used to procrastinate every time something needed to be done? In these, and countless other cases, the subconsciously driven or ingrained thoughts and behavior required no effort and—more importantly—*no thought* from our conscious mind.

You didn't have to consciously think to crack your knuckles or procrastinate when a thing needed to be done. Your subconscious mind took care of these thoughts and behaviors for you. However, when you decided to change these thoughts and behaviors, you had to use your conscious mind. You had to exert a great deal of effort.

Conscious thought requires effort—subconscious thought does not. As a result, everyone relies on their subconscious to do their thinking for them *as much as they can*.

The act of learning often requires conscious effort. Recall how difficult it was to learn to ride a bicycle or memorize the functions of a cellphone. However, once you learned to ride the bicycle or operate your phone, your subconscious mind assumed or took over these duties, freeing your conscious mind to think about anything you desire.

But learning does not always require a significant conscious effort. Often, learning requires *no conscious effort.* Consider the minimal effort to learn by reading when you are not consciously examining what you are reading. And consider that no effort is necessary to learn by way of observation.

Learning without the conscious mind is both a great strength and weakness. It is a strength because conscious thought requires effort, but it is also a weakness because the subconscious *cannot differentiate* fact from fiction, truth from falsehood. It passively absorbs information. As everyone relies on their subconscious to do their thinking for them as often as they can, we end up living the majority of our lives according to things we learned that we did not consciously examine for truth or falsehood—or the well or ill-being of our people.

Entertainment is the most powerful form of MP infection because the infection is received by the subconscious without conscious examination. What's worse, most people find it annoying to consciously examine entertainment while being entertained: *"There can't be any explosions in space. There isn't any oxygen." "An animal that large couldn't live in that setting. What would it eat?" "I don't care that she wears a cape. A human being can't fly."*

Want more proof that your subconscious is incapable of discerning fact from fiction and that your conscious mind isn't engaged while consuming entertainment? Think back to when you watched a dramatic scene in a movie—your heart raced as the suspense built. Recall your stomach turning when you read about a ship listing on rough seas. Remember your anger rising when the protagonist on a TV show was wronged by an unscrupulous adversary. You can consciously say that the book, TV show or movie is fiction, but your subconscious mind does not know the difference.

As a child—or even as an adult—have you ever had to remind yourself that the gore and slaughter on the screen wasn't real, or that the frightening movie you are watching is *only* a movie. Have you ever had to remind yourself that the impossible and terrifying characters and their fictional powers were not real to quell your rising anxiety? Have you ever walked around your home with a heightened sense of dread or fear for days after watching a horror movie? Were you ever afraid of a forest or an old house—or the old lady at the end of the street—because of what you saw in a movie or TV show?

These are examples of the *weakness* of the subconscious mind to discern fact from fiction and the *absolute power* it exercises over our lives. The lives we live in the real, non-fiction world are largely based on the fiction we consume. This is so important that I am going to write that sentence a second time: The lives we live in the real, non-fiction world are largely based on the fiction we consume.

Think about the language we use when we talk about fictional characters. *"He did that because his heart was broken." "She was obviously thinking only about herself when she made that decision." "Why would he act like that? I suppose he was under a lot of stress."* In all of these cases, the characters did what they did because they were *following a script.*

We consciously know that the actors are following a script, but our subconscious mind connects to the scripted, fictional characters as if they are real people with real lives and real motives for us to discern.

The fact that we have to *argue* with ourselves about the fear and ideas induced by fiction—that the *real forest* does not contain the monsters from the *fictional forest*, or that our homes do not contain the demons from the fictional houses, is evidence that *control over our identities, perception of the world, and our decisions* is split between the conscious and subconscious.

This reality has enormous implications for our lives. It means that what we consume as entertainment is far more decisive and important than what we eat and drink or take in the form of drugs and disease inoculations. It is far more important because what we consume as entertainment determines who we are as individuals and as a people.

The weakness of the subconscious mind makes it far more susceptible to MP infection, and it also exercises far more control over our beliefs, motivations, actions, and understandings of the world because we rely on it more often than our conscious mind to live our lives.

Now, let us apply these important facts to the matter at hand. Entertainment is a powerful force in shaping the subconscious mind. The subconscious mind is a powerful force in shaping your understandings and actions. So, how does the entertainment we are exposed to throughout our society shape our subconscious mind and thus our understanding and actions?

What does entertainment teach the Westman about himself and his people? What does it teach him about his past—and the past of other races? What does it teach him is moral and immoral? What does it train him to do or not to do?

Think about all of the books you've read (and had read to you as a child). Think of all the movies and TV shows you've watched. Think about the songs you've heard and sung along to in the car. Now, remember how the villainous Westmen characters injured innocent, virtuous nonwhites—how the white man who was concerned with the welfare of his people was the despised villain—how the Westmen succeeded only because he persecuted nonwhites—and on and on and on... and on.

Furthermore, when entertainment depicts attractive white actors who work against the well-being of Westernkind, receiving attention, love, wealth, sex, and prestige, we subconsciously learn to imitate that behavior in the expectation of those rewards.

When entertainment depicts unattractive white actors, concerned with and working for the well-being of Westernkind incurring hatred, humiliation, impoverishment, disgust, and ostracism we subconsciously learn to reject White Wellbeing in the vain hope that we will be spared the condemnation, **antiwhite slurs**, and punishments inflicted on our people.

These and many other MPs bypassed conscious examination. They were received by your subconscious, which is incapable of discerning fact from fiction. And as the subconscious "thinks" for us most of the time, these MPs shape your understanding of yourself, our people, history, and the present.

Meme-Pathogen Infection:

Multiracialism and

Bio-Spiritual Injury

How do we quantify the human soul? How does the human mind create consciousness? Answer these questions and you'll have the tools with which to fully understand the **bio-spirit**.

A bio-spirit is the (as yet) incomprehensible force unique to each people. Its mysteries can be crudely defined as instinct—the natural, historic, and expected thought and behavioral/personality patterns distinct to a people. Every people has a broadly recognizable expression. A people's **bio-spiritual expression** projected onto their environment is their **culture**.

How do we know that culture is the bio-spiritual projection of a race of people? We *see* it and we have *always seen* it. Westmen produce Western Civilization. Asians produce Asian Civilization. Africans produce African Civilization.

When Asians enclave in Western countries, they recreate Asiatic expressions, most clearly demonstrated in China Towns. Similarly, when Westmen enclave in Asian countries, they recreate Western expressions. Hong Kong is an example of Western businessmen influencing Asiatic bio-spiritual expression.

No one questions (or legitimately can question) that the races of humanity are different in measurable ways. All quantifiable human variation follows a standard distribution by race. These differences can be graphed and put on a bell-shaped curve. IQ, physiological and phenotypic markers, athletic ability, disease patterns and propensities, types and rates of crime, maturation rates, etc. can all be measured and clearly distinguishes the races of man. You will find that on every such graph (every quantifiable characteristic) that race is the key to understanding the results.

Why would the instincts of a people, their spiritual expression, their esthetic, their values, their passions, their motivations—in other words, their culture—be any different? *Culture is the culminating aggregate of a people's bio-spiritual expression projected onto their environment.*

The obvious question is: If culture is the projection of the bio-spirit of a people—and every people has their own unique bio-spirit—what is the result of different peoples living together in a single society? The answer is **bio-spiritual incompatibility**, which causes discomfort, disharmony, and conflict.

Bio-spiritual reflection is akin to the sun's light that bounces off the moon. Bio-spiritual reflection is the reflection of a people's bio-spirit. In a word, bio-spiritual reflection is a people's *culture*. In this analogy, the sun and the bio-spirit represent the source. The moon and the culture reflect toward the source.

Bio-spiritual harmony is the feelings of harmony, belonging, comfort, and spiritual enrichment that are induced when the reflection creates a feedback loop between a culture and a culture's creators.

Bio-spiritual disharmony is the feelings of disharmony, discomfort, alienation, and spiritual impoverishment that are induced when the cultural reflection is different from a people's bio-spirit.

This is why an environment resonates (physically, mentally, and spiritually) with the people who projected that expression—a feeling of being at home as opposed to a strange land. When people live in the societies they have created, they live in harmony with their creation. They live with natural familiarity and comfort. On the other hand, when a people live in a society that reflects alien bio-spiritual expression, they feel disharmony, unfamiliarity, and discomfort.

What is true of feeling at home or in a strange land because of the bio-spiritual reflection is also largely true of a people's ease or hardship—success or failure—in that society. When people live in societies they have created, they are successful in those societies. After all, they have created the frameworks, values, and systems according to their bio-spirit. On the other hand, when a people live in a society that reflects a different bio-spirit, they find it difficult to succeed. After all, they are trying to comply with goals, standards, and expectations that are alien to their bio-spirit.

Antiwhites correctly observe that nonwhites feel discomfort, live in disharmony, and have difficulty succeeding in Western countries. However, instead of understanding these as natural consequences of living in a culture made from incompatible bio-spiritual expressions, antiwhites incorrectly attribute the discomfort and failures of nonwhites to the "malevolence" of Westernkind.

They hold Westernkind responsible for the poor performance and bad behavior of nonwhites within white societies. The result is that antiwhites demand that Westmen alter their culture to be more comfortable for nonwhites, and they use **MIS** *pretexts*, such as *"the need for whites to be inclusive"* to inflict this harm on us. By altering and destroying that which we love, brings us pleasure, and secures our well-being, antiwhites inflict harm on our people and therefore us as individual Westmen.

As the nonwhite population grows in white countries and nonwhite **numerical courage** increases, our countries become increasingly inhospitable for us. Prior to achieving numerical courage, nonwhites are in a state of **numerical diffidence**. While in this state, nonwhites superficially conform to the bio-spiritual expression of Westernkind: standards, morality, behavioral norms and the like.

However, once numerical courage is achieved, nonwhites increasingly exert and impose their own bio-spiritual expressions on us and our society. This is why nonwhite enclaves take on the personalities of nonwhites, despite being surrounded by Western culture and structured with Western language, business, and legal systems.

At what population level numerical courage occurs is relative to a host of factors. It depends on things such as the nonwhite population's religious and cultural exhortations/traditions and racial enclaving. It also depends upon the strength or weakness of white unity. Numerical courage is harder to achieve in the presence of greater white unity. On the other hand, white disunity lowers the bar—and the requisite nonwhite population can be much smaller when it begins to reshape white culture into its own bio-spiritual expression.

It is clear from the way multiracial society functions that individual antiwhites need not plan, desire, or even consider **white erasure** to achieve white erasure. They need only inflict aggregate and cumulative harm on Westernkind. This is death by countless acts that harm us and alter our civilization. It is no wonder that so many whites around the Western world report that they feel like strangers in their own countries.

The more antiwhites white-guilt Westmen into permitting the alteration of our countries to suit the bio-spiritual preferences of nonwhites, the less our countries reflect our own bio-spiritual nature. This, of course, causes Westmen to feel out of place and uncomfortable. Mutual discomfort as a consequence of bio-spiritual incompatibility is a cause of great conflict. In cases where two or more peoples achieve numerical courage, the result is a *cultural arms race*, which causes governments to implement severe tyrannical efforts to spy on and punish the—increasingly—mutually antagonistic populations, and is the basis for violent balkanization.

Meme-Pathogen Infection:

Antiwhitism

and the

Antiwhite Narrative

Antiwhitism is all concepts, ideologies, actions and everything deriving therefrom (such as opinions, policies, laws, rules) that inflict injury on Westernkind and Western Civilization.

Antiwhites use carefully crafted pretexts to "justify" antiwhitism. These pretexts are classified as **MIS**: the **moralization, intellectualization, and sentimentalization** of the antiwhite desire to inflict harm on Westernkind. (Note: While all MPs are pretexts to arrive at antiwhite conclusions, not all MIS pretexts are MPs.)

Examples:

- All races are inherently equal (interchangeable). Thus, nonwhite lack of achievement is due to the "evil" and "selfishness" of white people; thus, all immigrants are the same; thus....

- Nonwhite children deserve white charity because their suffering is "caused" by whites, either because white people "created" the situations or "failed to correct" the situations that caused their suffering.
- Whites "owe" nonwhites entry into our countries because it accords with our moral obligation to do unto others as we would have done unto ourselves.
- There is no race but the "human race."
- Nonwhite racial quotas.
- "White privilege" college courses.
- Corporate "diversity" training programs.

As antiwhites and antiwhite doctrines predominate the news and entertainment media, governments, universities, and church leadership, the Antiwhite Narrative is the official narrative of Western Civilization—the daily, historical, civilizational story within which we live our lives. It is everything you know about the world beyond your immediate experiences with family, friends, and work.

The Antiwhite Narrative is fiction and is debunked by lived experience and unfiltered statistics. In addition to MPs and other tools of persuasion, antiwhites enforce the narrative by *stigmatizing*, *pathologizing*, and *criminalizing* everyone and everything that deviates from the Antiwhite Narrative. Conversely, those who articulate and enforce the Antiwhite Narrative are often rewarded for these antiwhite acts.

Antiwhites derive this narrative from antiwhitism and the application of **antiwhite lenses** to historical, contemporary, and forecasted events. Antiwhite lenses are derived from MIS pretexts and MPs.

Antiwhites use MIS pretexts, MPs, antiwhitism, interpretive mandates, and antiwhite lenses in circular reasoning to "prove" their arguments.

As such lenses are rooted in a deeply concealed **jealousy and envy** of Westernkind, they often conflict superficially. As a result, antiwhites appear to be internally conflicted and are often labeled hypocrites.

For example, antiwhites often attack wealth (*"Wealth is denied to nonwhites and used as a tool to suppress/exploit nonwhites"*). However, they celebrate wealthy antiwhites and the use of that wealth to suppress and exploit Westmen.

Externally, antiwhites appear hypocritical, but they are not internally conflicted and thus they are able to behave with the certainty of a religious zealot. In both cases (the condemning of wealth and the celebration of wealth), the true—unspoken—objective of harming Westernkind is served.

Seeing antiwhite "hypocrisy" is the first step, but the goal is to see that there is no hypocrisy.

Seeing is Believing:

Antiwhitism Throughout Society

In the following segments, you are introduced to MP identification and classification, an ability crucial to Going Free. You cannot cure yourself of an ailment if you do not identify and classify the ailment.

Antiwhitism is everywhere in Western Civilization. Unfortunately, its prevalence can make it difficult for Westmen to identify. Much like deep-sea fish submerged in the vastness of the ocean are unable to fathom a world beyond the water, Westmen submerged in antiwhitism can find it difficult to perceive the Antiwhite Narrative as something artificial, fictional, and harmful.

However, as with any skill, with time and practice you will improve your ability to identify and Go Free of MPs. And the more MPs you are able to identity, the more adept you become at identifying them. You will soon realize that you are no less submerged in antiwhite poison than deep-sea fish are submerged in the vastness of the ocean.

Antiwhitism in Commercials

We begin with commercials. These snapshots from our environment are loaded with antiwhitism. At first, they may seem like coincidences. But advertising decisions are never left to chance. The races of the actors, who is paired with whom, who is portrayed in a bad or good light, the music that is used for superiority and inferiority, are conscious decisions that—increasingly over the past few decades—prioritize antiwhitism over profit.

Keep in mind that antiwhites will dismiss individual examples of commercials as chance, but they cannot dismiss a holistic assessment of advertising across the West.

A toothpaste commercial with a beautiful white woman arm-in-arm with a nonwhite man. They are both laughing and smiling euphorically.

What messages does such imagery convey? If the goal were simply to encourage the viewer to buy toothpaste, any happy couple would do. What is the purpose of the interracial couple (a statistically miniscule percentage of couples)?

The commercial speaks to white women. It suggests that you are beautiful if you brush your teeth with the product in the commercial, but it also suggests that choosing a nonwhite man results in picture perfect love.

A car commercial compares two car buying experiences. One commercial shows a dumb white couple, ungroomed and badly dressed, buying an overpriced lemon from a sleazy car dealer. The other portrays a smart, stylishly dressed, nonwhite couple making the "right" choice and buying a fair-priced, superior automobile.

What MPs does this scenario convey? Nonwhite people are smart. They groom themselves, dress well, and they make intelligent decisions. White couples, by contrast, are out of shape slobs who are easily cheated.

A commercial for cereal opens in a beautiful kitchen. You find a family, happily enjoying breakfast. The carefully engineered lighting creates a warm, homey scene. The nonwhite husband and his white wife are proud of the intelligent questions their precocious, biracial child is asking over morning cereal.

What MPs does this commercial impart? White women prefer nonwhite men. White men, therefore, are inferior. White and nonwhite couples produce children who are just as clever as white children (probably more so). Interracial relationships create happy homes, strong marriages, and harmonious families.

A home security agency depicts white men breaking into a home. The nonwhite homeowner (or single white mother) calls the alarm company. A competent, nonwhite switchboard operator reassures her and a nonwhite police officer arrives to save the day.

What are the MPs? White men are criminals. Nonwhites are victims of white men. Nonwhites are the "good guys." White women should look to nonwhite men for protection from white men.

An insurance commercial uses human characteristics to pitch its protection. The heroic insurance company is personified as a nonwhite man. The nonwhite man protects you from "mayhem," which is personified by a white man.

What are the MPs in this commercial? Mayhem, misfortune, and disaster are associated with Westernkind in general and white men specifically. On the other hand, protection, dependability, and assistance are associated with nonwhites in general and nonwhite men specifically.

A radio commercial uses a white man affecting a goofy voice to represent an inferior product sold at an excessive price. He is contrasted by the soothing, deep voice of a nonwhite man offering a superior product at a fair price.

What MPs does this radio commercial impart? White men are goofy and dishonest. Nonwhite men, like the product represented by the nonwhite actor, are superior.

*A clothing advertisement in a newspaper or
magazine: Two, stylish couples strut down a
street for a fabulous night out on the town. There
are four actors—two white and two nonwhite.
Both couples are interracial.*

What MPs does this advertisement send? Whites should date nonwhites to have fun and be modern/stylish. Stylish and "acceptable" whites prefer to date nonwhites. White men are inferior to nonwhite men and white women are inferior to nonwhite women. Attractive and successful whites choose nonwhite mates.

What were some of the MPs in the previous examples?

- White men are criminals.
- White men are stupid and naive.
- White men are shysters.
- Successful white women prefer nonwhite men.
- Successful white men prefer nonwhite women.
- It is more fun and stylish to be with nonwhites.
- White women should look to nonwhite men for protection.
- Interracial families are successful, happy, and harmonious.

Your Examples of Antiwhitism in Commercials

In your own words, give three examples of antiwhitism/Antiwhite Narrative in print, radio, or television commercials:

Antiwhitism in Entertainment

The entertainment media—popular fiction, stage, screen, and television—abound with MPs.

Heroes and Villains

Villains are nearly always Westmen. If there are nonwhite villains, they have a sympathetic backstory, are forced by circumstances (caused by Westmen) into a life of crime, and/or they are working for the true villain, who is a Westman.

The heroes crucial to the triumph of good over the white villain are played by a multiracial cast.

We learn that whites are inherently villainous and nonwhites are inherently virtuous. Whites can only be *good* when siding with nonwhites against other whites. Westmen need nonwhite support to make them whole, valuable, and correct.

Leaders and Geniuses

Nonwhites are cast in the roles of intellectually superior characters: the genius, scientist, professor, judge, president, even God. White actors are cast as the intellectually inferior characters, who are amazed by the insights, brilliance, and leadership of the nonwhites.

Westmen should look to nonwhites for solutions. In fact, nonwhites are so perfectly competent that white disagreement is likely driven by prejudice rather than objective analysis. Westmen are submissive and surrender authority to nonwhites because nonwhites have the answers and know how to lead.

The effects of this MP are easily seen in the real world of sociopolitical advocacy. Most whites are uncomfortable endorsing or participating in causes that lack nonwhite support and participation. They feel an urge to include nonwhites. This is because they know (subconsciously or consciously) that their opinions are suspect without significant nonwhite agreement. Such beliefs are engendered by this and other MPs.

At a subconscious level, they feel that whites working toward a goal without nonwhite participation is somehow wrong. They are relieved if a nonwhite expresses agreement, and often clamor for such nonwhites to assume high-profile roles. [What do you call the only black man at a conservative gathering? *"The keynote speaker."*]

Women and the Men They Should Seek

MPs that show nonwhite men as intellectually superior leaders and heroes encourage white women to see nonwhite men as superior mates. There are numerous MPs that are designed *specifically* to urge white women to favor nonwhite men over their own men.

Entertainment depicts white men as intrinsically awkward, clumsy, and unpolished. On the other hand, nonwhite men are portrayed as naturally suave, hip, and stylish. White men may be able to learn to be cool or hip— but only by mimicking nonwhites and nonwestern behaviors. White women are depicted as impressed by nonwhite males, vying for their attention.

There is a particularly insidious collection of MPs directed at white women and intended to influence them to seek nonwhite mates. These MPs cause white women to fear white men and see nonwhite men as protectors of women and children.

Think about how many movies are about white, clean-cut, and educated men who are secretly ruthless abusers or serial killers of women. By contrast, how many movies have you seen where nonwhite men, despite their apparent thuggishness, are actually kind, sympathetic, considerate, and natural protectors of women and children?

The clean-cut, intelligent Westman is a benign façade for a monster lurking underneath. The thuggish nonwhite man is a rough exterior for a misunderstood heart of gold.

These MPs infect white women with the notion that exterior signals are untrustworthy—and are likely to run contrary to a person's real identity. A white woman's white neighbor may be well spoken and have a history of good deeds, but he is potentially a predator. By contrast, her nonwhite neighbor may have a record of violence, crime, and misdeeds—but he is likely a good person.

Dead White Souls and Nonwhite Spirituality

Entertainment consistently shows nonwhites as in-touch with God and more attuned to mystical nature than Westmen. Westmen are soulless materialists—severed from a vast and unseen supernatural knowledge and power. Nonwhites have a special ability—absent in whites—that enables them to access this supernatural reservoir of knowledge and power. Nonwhites are far closer to the divine than is possible for Westmen.

White Genocidal Maniacs and Nonwhite Good Samaritans

Westmen persecute, trick, and exploit others (especially nonwhites). Nonwhites live in harmony with all peoples. Whereas Westmen have been uniquely harmful toward other races, nonwhites help and never harm outsiders.

When the entertainment script shows peoples in conflict, nonwhites are depicted as noble self-defenders. Westmen are always depicted as ignoble, genocidal maniacs. In fact, any concern for White Wellbeing is, by definition, wicked. Consequently, all whites who are concerned with the well-being of Westernkind are villains.

Related to the MPs that reinforce concern for White Wellbeing as being immoral and evil are the MPs that go deeper—the MPs that teach Westmen that opposing White Wellbeing is noble and praiseworthy. Whites are "good" if they fight against their own kind. To be antiwhite is to fight "immorality" and "evil."

Your Examples of Antiwhitism in Entertainment

In your own words, give three examples of antiwhitism/Antiwhite Narrative in entertainment:

Antiwhitism in the News

Called by many names: "dinosaur media," "fakestream," "lamestream," "mainstream," "establishment," "state," and "controlled," the news media is part of the Regime, which is composed of the news and entertainment media, governments, academia as well as the banks and all institutions influenced by these entities. Regime created and approved "news" is processed through antiwhite lenses to ensure that it conforms to the Antiwhite Narrative.

The Regime Casts the Characters and Writes the "News" Scripts

Regime news media fabricate "news." Like fiction writers, Regime media employees use events and facts of events to write scripts. The degree to which these fictions approach reality depends on the relationship between the event/facts and the Antiwhite Narrative. Events and facts of events that disconfirm or can be made to appear to confirm the Antiwhite Narrative are more likely to be fictionalized.

The objective of Regime media employees is to "prove" the Antiwhite Narrative with unethical antiwhite interpretations, omissions, fabrications and deliberate misrepresentations of actual events. This soap opera is formulaic.

Events or facts of events that do not conform to the Antiwhite Narrative are ignored, suppressed, or inverted (disconfirming events or facts are inverted to confirm the Antiwhite Narrative). Events or facts of events that can be made to appear supportive of the Antiwhite Narrative are magnified, written into "news" scripts, and disseminated to the public. Antiwhites in the Regime media will also falsify events and facts of events to "prove" the Antiwhite Narrative.

Let's look at how crime is reported. The script is written in one of two ways dependent upon the race of the wrongdoer and victim. It begins by cherry picking and misrepresenting actual events. When whites commit crime, the Regime focuses coverage on these crimes and sensationalizes the white criminals as "ultimate villains." The Regime then extrapolates the unethical and criminal behaviors of the white wrongdoer and applies them to all of Westernkind—and therefore you as a Westman.

Every time a crime by a Westman against a nonwhite presents an opportunity to "prove" the Antiwhite Narrative, the Regime news spurs public debate with *"conversations about race and hate."* And these conversations always have one conclusion—Westernkind is an evil people, victimizing innocent nonwhites.

On the other hand, when nonwhites commit crime, the crimes go unreported; or receive far less coverage, with the racial dynamics de-emphasized or ignored, particularly when the victims are white. Often, nonwhite criminals are portrayed as "tragic" cases: *"victims of society,"* and therefore *"victims of Westernkind."*

Nonwhite crime, therefore, is excused or rationalized with a host of MPs, such as *"systemic racism."* How many times have you heard Regime media report or host a pundit who justifies nonwhite crime with a *false equivalency* of crimes committed by nonwhites and the "racism" that "caused" the criminality? Not only is nonwhite criminality excused, but—*again*—the entirety of Westernkind is blamed.

Westman commits crime=Westernkind is blamed.

Nonwhite commits crime=Westernkind is blamed.

This careful and dishonest narrative-shaping warps perception of the world. Westmen believe that the white crime rate and threat to public safety by Westernkind are greater than the objective data shows—and what their own eyes reveal (See *The Color of Crime* statistical analysis of crime, available free on the American Renaissance website).

Likewise, Westmen believe that the nonwhite crime rate and threat to public safety are less than objective data shows—and what their common sense perceives. This warping of reality convinces many of our people that we are inherently evil and that nonwhites are inherently innocent and virtuous.

In addition to deciding what stories do or do not make the news and how the participants are going to be portrayed, there are a thousand tricks the Regime media use to "prove" the Antiwhite Narrative.

Listen to any Regime media report, and you will find that under the guise of reporting news, "news" script writers are actually editorializing with carefully chosen adjectives, emotional pauses, and concerned cadences.

"News reporters" interview pundits who are "experts." Reporters feed these pundits carefully selected questions and provide the platform of "objective news" for these antiwhites to "prove" the Antiwhite Narrative.

A Case Study of Regime News: George Zimmerman and Treyvon Martin

The Regime's news coverage of the Treyvon Martin case is a perfect encapsulation of these strategies. The narrative that antiwhites wanted Americans to believe was: *"Racist white man murders innocent black child in cold blood."*

Racist White Man:

George Zimmerman, the man who shot Treyvon Martin, was consistently referred to as a "white man" and "white Hispanic man" instead of the norm when referring to nonwhite Hispanics as *Hispanic*. There were also cases of Regime media outlets lightening his photograph to make him appear white. And, until they were exposed, NBC unethically edited the original 911 emergency call to make the shooter and the shooting appear to be racially motivated.

Black Child:

Every Regime outlet used out-of-date photographs of Martin. These old photographs portrayed Martin as a small, innocent, smiling, prepubescent child.

The reality was that Treyvon Martin was a large, 6' tall, robust, high school football player. Only alternative media outlets showed current photographs of Martin posing aggressively with various *gangsta* props and displaying gang gestures. And, let us not forget the endless reportage the Regime gave to antiwhite President Obama's comment, *"If I had a son, he'd look like Treyvon."*

Innocent Black Child—Cold Blooded White Murderer:

The Regime used falsified 911 tapes to paint the nonwhite George Zimmerman as a "white racist" on the prowl to "lynch" black children: Westernkind=evil, nonwhites=innocent victims.

At the same time, the Regime worked to deflect or entirely suppress Zimmerman's account that he acted in self-defense. Zimmerman stated (and a forensic pathologist testified that Zimmerman's statements were supported by the evidence) that Martin was on top of Zimmerman and bashing his head repeatedly into the concrete.

These antiwhite tactics to "prove" the Antiwhite Narrative cause our people to question our own observations of white and nonwhite crime. This "proof" causes our people to feel compassion and sympathy for nonwhite criminals, to feel white-guilt for a nonwhite criminal's choice to victimize the innocent.

We are crippled with an antiwhite vocabulary and perspective that undermine our efforts to champion White Wellbeing. We are inundated with "authorities" and "experts" who chastise us, especially **white sympathetic** Westmen, as immoral.

And, as Regime media control the framing of all events and the facts of events, the Regime also builds fear in our people. This fear causes many Westmen to police their own thoughts and behaviors so as not to be targeted and victimized by antiwhites.

In recent years, a number of factors have eroded the absolute control that Regime media once held over framing events to conform to the Antiwhite Narrative. In response, antiwhites have resorted to building imitation alternative news sources, which are created to gain the trust of viewers who have become skeptical of Regime reportage.

These "alternative outlets" criticize Regime media, but these imposters can always be identified by their conclusions, which are directly or indirectly favorable to the Regime and conform to the Antiwhite Narrative.

Your Examples of Antiwhitism in the News

In your own words, give three examples of antiwhitism/Antiwhite Narrative in the news:

Antiwhitism in Academia

Academia is the Regime-subsidized or influenced education that is pervaded with antiwhitism—intolerance, pseudoscience, pseudo-logic, superstition and suppression of dissent.

The MPs and antiwhite tactics listed below are a representative, but in no way exhaustive, catalog of antiwhitism in academia:

- *Moralizes, intellectualizes,* and *sentimentalizes* (MIS) antiwhite jealousy, envy, covetousness, hatred of and the infliction of harm on Westernkind. Examples: *"structural racism"* and *"the gender pay gap."*

- Suppresses history, science, and data that undermine the Antiwhite Narrative. Examples: suppression of crime and IQ differences among the races. Suppression of evidence indicating that Westernkind may have been the first people in the Americas (Solutrean hypothesis), as explored by Dennis Stanford, archaeologist and Director of the Paleoindian/Paleoecology Program at the National Museum of Natural History at the Smithsonian in Washington D.C.

- Invents/distorts "history," science, and data to "prove" the Antiwhite Narrative. Examples: *"Christopher Columbus genocided Amerindians." "South Africa is a harmonious multiracial society after whites turned over the control of their country to antiwhite nonwhites."*

- Suppresses all attempts to investigate, criticize, or disprove the Antiwhite Narrative. Examples: stigmatizing such endeavors as unethical and/or blocking such efforts with various institutional codes, publication bias, defunding efforts and similar underhandedness.

- Constructs and teaches concepts, words, and phrases designed to support and "prove" the Antiwhite Narrative. Examples: *"white privilege," "legacy of slavery."*

- Constructs and teaches concepts, words, and phrases designed to hamper, undermine, and pathologize defense of Westernkind and Western Civilization. Examples: *"check your privilege," "racism."*

- Attributes straw man arguments to advocates of White Wellbeing. Examples: **white positive** advocates want to *"nullify interracial marriages"* and *"sterilize handicapped people."*

- Misrepresents white positive positions. Examples: White Wellbeing advocates want to abolish racial quotas in hiring *"so that they can return to bigoted hiring practices."* White Wellbeing advocates claim to care about White Wellbeing *"but what they really mean is that they want white supremacy."*

- Serves as a training ground for antiwhite radicalization. Examples: university funded antiwhite workshops, symposiums, and graduate degrees in *"social justice and activism."*

- Serves as indoctrination centers for white-guilting whites and engendering white self-hate. Examples: many universities require *all* students to take classes about *"white privilege"* and *"racism"* to graduate. Most curricula contain a racial subtext that conforms to the Antiwhite Narrative.

<u>Your Examples of Antiwhitism in Academia</u>

In your own words, give three examples of antiwhitism/Antiwhite Narrative in academia:

Antiwhitism in Government

Antiwhitism is rampant in the federal, state and local governments of the West. A few examples:

- Affirmative action policies that legalize discrimination against whites for the advancement, enrichment, and empowerment of nonwhites in educational enrollment, hiring, promotions, government contracting, loans, grants, licensures, etc.

- Race-norming policies that exaggerate nonwhite performance by way of various and unscrupulous mechanisms, thereby undermining white effort and achievement. For example, artificially inflating admission test scores for nonwhites.

- Taxation policies that disproportionately affect or harm whites while benefiting nonwhites. For example, antiwhite dominated governments inflating property values in white areas in order to increase the tax revenue from those areas. These funds are then lavished on nonwhites and nonwhite areas.

- Failure to enforce laws that (intentionally and unintentionally) accrue to the benefit of Westmen.

For example, laws protecting the nation's borders from illegal nonwhite immigration.

- Immigration and welfare policies that prioritize and fast-track nonwhite applicants while retarding and protracting the process for white applicants.

- Changing the names of roads, schools, and landmarks that honor Westmen to supplant these celebrated whites with nonwhites and antiwhites (both nonwhite and white).

- Selective application of rules, laws, exemptions, waivers, and subsidies on the basis of race for the benefit of nonwhites and the detriment of whites. For example, the refusal of the Regime to enforce laws when nonwhites loot, riot, and commit **hate hoaxes**. By contrast, the Regime has illegally shut down legally and constitutionally permitted rallies organized by advocates for White Wellbeing.

Your Examples of Antiwhitism in Government

In your own words, give three examples of antiwhitism/Antiwhite Narrative in government:

Antiwhitism in Private Industry

and Associations

Antiwhitism pervades all areas of our lives. Our workplaces and social networks exhibit some of the harshest antiwhitism. In these places, forced "diversity" and "sensitivity" training white-guilt and indoctrinate Westmen, **antiwhite tribunals** are held, and **social lynchings** are perpetrated.

"Diversity and Sensitivity Training" programs are becoming ubiquitous in workplaces, schools, and social organizations across the Western world. These programs largely consist of browbeating and intimidating Westmen, while indulging and pampering nonwhites.

Likewise, antiwhite tribunals are now part of the human resources departments of most organizations. Antiwhite tribunals are the meetings/hearings wherein "bias incidents" or claims of "racism" are adjudicated. In these hearings, Westmen are interrogated, terrorized, humiliated, and punished for expressing/holding opinions at variance with antiwhitism (or merely refusing to express agreement with antiwhitism).

Social lynchings are becoming common place. Employees, students, and members of social networks who hold opinions that deviate from antiwhitism are socially lynched. Antiwhites zealously attack those who express (even unintentionally) opinions incompatible with the Antiwhite Narrative. These assaults consist of antiwhite slurs and economic, social, and psychological attacks.

Social lynching often results in alienation from family and friends. It can also mean a loss of employment (and all of the associated losses, such as loss of health insurance, one's ability to pay one's mortgage, auto, food, electricity payments, etc.).

Thankfully, the verbal framework of Going Free wards against social lynching, as well as providing appropriate responses to it.

This increasingly complex and multifaceted system of *engineering submission* to antiwhitism is designed to deter and punish dissent. In addition to these systemic antiwhite techniques, there are a great many specific actions taken within the private sphere that undermine Westernkind.

- Hiring, acceptance, and promotion policies that humiliate, demoralize, and exclude Westmen by discriminating against them to satisfy antiwhite goals, such as racial quotas and "diversification" objectives.

- School boards and parent-teacher organizations that advocate the replacement of Western heroes and the celebration of Western accomplishments with (often dubious) nonwhite and antiwhite (both white and nonwhite) heroes and accomplishments.

- Political organizations that betray their overwhelmingly white supporters by appointing nonwhites (on the basis of race) to positions of leadership, while also refusing to act for the well-being of whites.

- The religious organization or pastor who demoralizes and deceives his white congregants by preaching MPs as *"the word of God."*

Your Examples of Antiwhitism in
Private Industry and Associations

In your own words, give three examples of antiwhitism/Antiwhite Narrative in private industry and associations:

Antiwhitism in Family, Friendships, and Acquaintances

Even our personal relationships—from casual to intimate—are fraught with antiwhitism. The same kinds of social lynching used against Westmen who do not perfectly comply with the Antiwhite Narrative are perpetrated within families, friendships, and social networks.

Often, those we are closest to demand antiwhite conformity and punish deviation from the Antiwhite Narrative. Likewise, many of our personal relationships and social networks require antiwhite "virtue signaling," which we refer to as **villainy signaling**, as a form of *social payment*.

Even our most intimate and meaningful relationships are severed by whites who are so infected with MPs that they would rather destroy such relationships—marriages, families with children—than deviate from antiwhitism.

What follows are a representative handful of antiwhite festering wounds on our personal relationships:

- The parents who demand antiwhite conformity from their children and punish deviation.

- The acquaintance who villainy signals homage to antiwhitism and demands the same from you.
- The friend who looks for villainy signaling as a prerequisite for friendship.
- The girlfriend or boyfriend who blames and shames for deviation from antiwhitism.
- The priggish mother-in-law who condescendingly pontificates MPs at the dinner table.
- The aloof father-in-law who snubs you because of your lack of antiwhite belief.
- The sister/sister-in-law or brother/brother-in-law who brings a nonwhite date to family functions—stifling discussions that *might be* construed as offensive by a hypersensitive nonwhite.
- The daughter or son who, after a lifetime of MPs, turns against her/his parents and people.
- The neighbors and colleagues who expect you to grovel or pander to nonwhites.
- The online trolls who mock the suffering of Westernkind, deny white erasure, and harass you for dissenting from antiwhitism.

Your Examples of Antiwhitism in
Family, Friendships, and Acquaintances

In your own words, give three personal examples of antiwhitism/Antiwhite Narrative in your relationships with family, friends, and acquaintances:

The Path to Becoming an Antiwhite

We all have felt jealousy and envy—all of us—especially when we were children: Even if you were the most attractive, you were not the best musician, or the tallest, or the.... Even if you were the wealthiest, you were not the healthiest, or the smartest, or the....

The best of us use jealousy and envy to spur our efforts to equal or transcend the things that inspired these sentiments. And when nothing constructive can be done to equal or transcend the things that inspired these sentiments, we mature by coming to terms with reality: We can improve our appearance, but few of us will become models. We can increase our wealth, but few of us will become millionaires.

However, some people do not handle jealousy and envy well. A poisonous flame of resentment is ignited in the hearts of such people. They aim their resentment—like a loaded rifle—at all those for whom they feel jealousy and envy.

As a society, we condemn jealousy and envy, so those who hold these poisonous flames of resentment grope to justify their prohibited sentiments. The keepers of such resentment are exceedingly susceptible to creating and adopting ideas, excuses, and ideologies that justify and legitimize their secret resentment. And more importantly, they are exceedingly susceptible to ideologies and organizing principles that "right the wrongs" of the things that inspired their resentment. Antiwhitism speaks to these unhealthy sentiments, and promises to "right the wrongs."

"Equality" is the demand of he who measures his weaknesses against the strengths of others. With "equality," he publicly justifies his unprincipled resentment.

Both white and nonwhite antiwhites begin their sickness from the same place: jealousy and envy. When they look at the grandeur of Western Civilization, the beauty of Westernkind, and the glory of the West's history, they feel jealousy and envy.

The antiwhite nonwhite feels this way because he is not a Westman and thus not an inheritor of the dignity that our heritage bestows upon us. The antiwhite Westman feels this way because he does not see himself as a member of our people—and thus not an inheritor of our dignity: he might fixate on his wealth compared to our wealthiest, his intelligence compared to our most intelligent, his attractiveness compared to our most attractive, his talents compared to our most talented, his health compared to our healthiest, his humble upbringing compared to our most advantaged.

Jealousy and envy highlight the disparity between these individuals and Westernkind, and they call the disparity *injustice*, defining themselves as *victims*.

But who's to blame? Fate? Chance? God? Antiwhites cannot satisfy the desire for "revenge" on abstractions or deities, but they can "avenge" themselves on Westmen, who by virtue of their existence "cause" and "benefit from" the "injustice"—who by virtue of their existence are avatars for Westernkind.

In this way, antiwhites recast every Westman as an avatar for every strength against which the antiwhite measured himself to be weak: Every Westman represents greater wealth, even if he is poorer. Every Westman represents greater advantage, even if he is disadvantaged. Every Westman represents greater beauty, even if he is ugly.

This is the true aim of the antiwhite:

To "punish" the Westman for the feelings of inferiority that Westernkind inspires in him.

As (self-conceived) "victims," antiwhites gain the "right of self-defense," which enables them to *inflict harm* on Westmen in *good conscience*—and, which justifies the most fanatical behavior and actions. However, jealousy and envy are not legally, socially, or morally acceptable grounds for revenge in Western Civilization.

Antiwhites overcome this barrier with the *moralization, intellectualization,* and *sentimentalization* (MIS) of *pretexts* to "legitimize" the harm they inflict on Westmen.

These pretexts form the doctrine of antiwhitism, which the resentful among us fanatically adopt to serve their self-interest. Combined with the power of our leading institutions, which the antiwhites have hijacked, the antiwhites have established our modern, antiwhite "moral" code—MPs.

This power and "moral" code enables antiwhites to extort money, sex, resources, privileges and more from whites. Thus, the motivators *plunder* and *lust* are added to jealousy and envy.

Armed and motivated, antiwhites inflict harm on Westmen and attack Westernkind's bio-spiritual expressions—the culmination of which is Western Civilization. By altering and destroying that which we love, brings us happiness, and secures our well-being, antiwhites further inflict harm on our people.

A final note: individual antiwhites need not plan, desire, or even consider white erasure to achieve that outcome. They need only inflict aggregate and cumulative harm.

When You Go Free,

Who and What are You?

When you begin Going Free, your speech is white positive speech. Your actions are **white positive** actions. **White Wellbeing** matters to you. You are concerned with your own, your family's, and your friends' health and welfare, and you know that these things cannot be achieved—in any lasting and meaningful way—in the absence of our people's health and welfare.

Unlike the antiwhites who may temporarily advance, enrich, and empower nonwhites through the victimization and ruination of Westernkind (and therefore you as a Westman), your service to White Wellbeing is a service to the planet and all living organisms and peoples.

Ultimately, antiwhitism harms everyone and everything; therefore, opposition to it is a service to humanity and the world.

Antiwhites will identify you with antiwhite slurs, such as "racist" and "fascist," and demonized labels, such as "populist," "3rd positionist," "white nationalist" and "nationalist." But DO NOT adopt demonized labels. You are a Westman (a white man, woman or child) and a patriotic citizen of your country—nothing more or less. If you have previously labeled yourself with demonized labels, now is the time to drop the labels. To you, the labels of your choice had positive and fair meanings, but to the world's masses, such labels represent a host of meanings, motivations, and goals that are all objectionable and even evil—and *you* are none of those things.

Moreover, the antiwhite governments of the West increasingly add such labels to domestic terror lists. To self-identify as a label on one of those lists is to—by legal definition—identify as a domestic terrorist. You are practicing the practice of Going Free, a practice that is to the mind and soul of Westernkind what nutrition and exercise is to the body.

The antiwhite will object to your service to White Wellbeing by saying that *"We should care about everyone's well-being."* You agree. We should. There are thousands of groups serving Jewish Wellbeing, Black Wellbeing, Hispanic Wellbeing, Asian Wellbeing, Arab Wellbeing, and you are doing the same for White Wellbeing.

The antiwhite should celebrate and endorse your concern for White Wellbeing as much as he celebrates and endorses the well-being of nonwhite groups—but he won't, which reveals his pretext about *"caring for all peoples"* for what it actually is: an attempt to get you to surrender your service to White Wellbeing so that he and others can continue victimizing us.

Penniless whites are as penniless as penniless nonwhites. Whites suffering from disease suffer just as much as diseased nonwhites. Whites who cannot find employment are just as unemployed as unemployed nonwhites. And such white people are found in every county, city, state, and country across the West.

In fact, it is far worse for Westmen. The laws of our countries make us the only group that can be legally discriminated against in every area of life. The Antiwhite Narrative, which establishes the "morality" of the West, defines discrimination as commendable when it advances, enriches, and empowers nonwhites at our expense.

Does the antiwhite object to you improving yourself by *Going Free of antiwhite ideas and behaviors* that undermine your life? Does he object to you working to put an end to laws, rules, codes, and "moral" frameworks that unfairly inflict harm on innocent Westmen?

Does he object to you protecting white children from the cruelest child abuse the world has ever known, a child abuse that teaches them that they are descendants of an evil people and that they are only capable of redemption by working to **white-erase** their own kind?

You are white positive. You **serve White Wellbeing**. Anyone who disagrees with you serves **white ill-being** to various degrees and is probably antiwhite. When it comes to vagues, the choice is theirs: to commend you as they commend all nonwhites who strive to preserve and protect their own kinds, or to reveal that they are antiwhite by wanting all that is good for nonwhites while wanting—or at best being indifferent to—all that is bad for whites.

The Vague

The word **vague** is used here as a noun (rather than an adjective) to describe a type of person. Like the adjectival form of the word vague, the meanings *unclear*, *confused*, and *wavering* also apply to the noun form: a vague.

There are two types of vagues. The first are those who have not come into contact with antiwhitism, as might be found in rural China. The second are those who are not firmly antiwhite but who speak, write, and act (**villainy signal**) in ways that conform to the Antiwhite Narrative.

The second type of vague is referred to by large parts of the general public as a "normie," "lemming," "NPC" (non-player character), and "sheep." By way of their submission to the Antiwhite Narrative, these vagues constitute a subversive force to Westernkind and Western Civilization.

However, they have little to no understanding of the Regime and its antiwhite objectives. As this second category of vagues are passively complicit in the spread, legitimization, and enforcement of antiwhitism, they are often suspicious of those Going Free. They fear breaking from the herd, but they are the people, the brothers and sisters, whom we need to help Go Free.

Finally, we do not use the terms "normie," "lemming," "NPC," and "sheep" for various reasons: We subconsciously identify as abnormal when we use "normie." We are the normal, healthy members of our community. Using "lemming," "NPC," and "sheep" imply that such people are unwilling or unable to know the truth or do what is right, which engenders disgust in us rather than the love we should feel when trying to help them Go Free.

The Saboteur

Saboteurs come in numerous forms, several of which are given titles in the following paragraphs. They are marked by their negative influence on **white sympathetic communities**, including practitioners of Going Free.

Saboteurs may intentionally or unintentionally inflict their negative influence. They often engage in several types of **road blocking**, such as **virtue trapping**, **support shaming**, **spousing**, **shame extorting**, and **quicksanding** (a practice identified by Jared George).

The first type of saboteur is the **mercenary**, which has its own three variants. Least often, mercenaries are **professional agents**, members of antiwhite operations designed to infiltrate white sympathetic communities for the purpose of gathering intelligence, provoking violence, false flag operations and the like. These mercenaries are often government and NGO/private organization employees, but can also be contractors.

The second type of mercenary is the self-serving **opportunist**, joining or befriending white sympathetic communities with the intent of severing ties and "telling their story" for attention and financial reward from an antiwhite world eager to bolster the Antiwhite Narrative.

In this context, the **repentant villain** represents the third type of mercenary.

Whether leaving the group of their own volition or rejected for their aberrant behavior and ideas, they may reveal a mercenary side by not only seeking attention and acceptance, but also financial gain through "telling their story" about playing the villain in the Antiwhite Narrative.

Wellbeing advocates should stay vigilant of such individuals, who have caused harm to many other white sympathetic communities time and again. Be cautious of individuals lacking sincere dedication, study of the Going Free material, and positive participation.

After mercenaries are **cravens**, who encourage **white flight** and draw Wellbeing advocates away from our growing community by various means. One form of craven is the man or woman who enters the community for the purpose of **spousing** i.e. finding a quality mate and then luring that person away from White Wellbeing with various promises: a "peaceful life," sex, etc.

More often, cravens are **isolationists**, luring others into a *bunker mindset*: Cutting them off from the world; focusing their problem-solving thoughts, time, energy, and efforts on hunkering down for protracted societal collapse and personal siege; appealing to the basest of people's instincts—fear and panic; undermining their ability to spread Going Free and therefore the recapture of our destiny.

It should be noted that our individual well-being depends on our people's well-being. Bunker cravens rely on others, such as ourselves, to defeat the antiwhites and rebuild society. If we failed, the bunkers built by such cravens would, as one brilliant member of our community remarked, be no more than elaborate mausoleums.

Cravens and craven mentality must be swiftly resisted. Publicly identify these thoughts and individuals for what they are: cowardly, suicidal, indifferent to the suffering of others.

Prepping for natural or even man-made short-term stoppages or shortfalls in the normal functioning of society should not be confused with craven mentality. Such prepping steps are advisable in light of hostile antiwhite sentiment and "equality/equity" replacing competence in all spheres of society.

Abstractionists and **sectarianists** are two other forms of saboteurs. An abstractionist places more value on the abstractions created by a people, such as *"equality before the law"*, than he places on the people who created the abstractions.

To do so is to sacrifice the creators on the altar of their ideas, a supremely immoral act. Our abstractions do not exist without us, and what will it matter in the scale of human tragedy if they persist after our **biological white erasure**? Examples of abstractionist thought are libertarianism, conservatism, communism, etc.

Sectarianists disunify. They magnify differences that are either trivial or out of turn, demanding reconciliation of various elements before reconciliation or resolution is necessary—even before it is known that reconciliation or resolution will be necessary in the future. They spread rumors and instigate personal grievances. They praise one and denounce the other, and in various ways seek to unnecessarily fracture strength and united effort. Both abstractionists and sectarianists can act with malice aforethought, but they are as likely to be driven by MPs and/or low intelligence.

Finally, the **antagonist** is another saboteur. He *plays the villain* in the Antiwhite Narrative.

The antagonist derives his name from the assortment of villains (antagonists) presented by the Antiwhite Narrative: entertainment, "historical" edutainment and much more. These fictional and fictionalized characters are portrayed as representing the worst qualities of humanity and then infused with some measure of concern for or fixation on the white race. They are adorned with demonized symbols (or their symbols are malevolently redefined), given vile speech (or their speech maliciously misrepresented), and animated with destructive behaviors (or deceitfully blamed).

When a white man, woman, or child decides to give his or her life in selfless sacrifice to the well-being of our people, that is a pristine moment of purest love, courage, and nobility; however, such heroes are trapped within the Antiwhite Narrative (which they believe is reality), where their choices for white positive thought and action are limited to imitations of the antagonist characters within the Antiwhite Narrative.

Disgusted by antiwhites playing the victim, the antagonist doubles down when playing the villain. Personal historical research and other factors often result in deep loyalties to forms, thoughts, and expressions of concern for our people that have been irredeemably demonized.

Such people should not cast (what they believe to be their pearls) before the "swine" of the public. Rather, if they believe they have discovered hidden or slandered truths, they must place these venerated thoughts and things in private, honored places, and reconnect with their original pristine moment of purest love, courage, and nobility by Going Free and serving White Wellbeing.

The Repentant Villain

As noted above, two character roles depicted within the Antiwhite Narrative and adopted in the real world are the villain and the **repentant villain**. Whereas the villain is the antagonist, the repentant villain is not necessarily the reverse.

The repentant villain has merely dropped one prepared role for another. Most often, the repentant villain feels remorse; he regrets some or most of the speech, ideas, and behaviors that characterized who he was when he played the villain. Such repentant villains often quietly drop out of white sympathetic activities, groups and relationships.

Occasionally, the repentant villain becomes a saboteur. Driven by mercenary greed and/or antiwhite fanaticism, he seeks attention/acceptance and/or financial gain by way of antiwhite speech and behavior as well as "telling his story."

There is likely some degree of repentant villain in the heart of every Westman playing the villain. The antagonist role does not comport with our bio-spirit. It is not natural for Westmen to think and act outside of an objective moral matrix. Such internal conflict is probably the cause of most of the childish tantrums that antagonists are known for.

Thought Leaders in the

White Sympathetic Sphere

Whether leading organizational entities or providing edutainment, thought leaders in the **white sympathetic sphere** are either **doom documenters** or **doom dissectors**; they either report on the harm that antiwhites are inflicting on Westernkind and Western Civilization, or they search through contemporary/historical events and disciplines, only tenuously relevant to our situation, for deeper meaning as well as the formulating of new questions to stimulate further inquiry.

Often, doom documenters specialize in entertaining you, some by way of sharing the most sensational, mysterious and infuriating acts of doom, and others by way of punctuating their doom documenting with flippancy, jocularity, and crude jokes.

Doom dissectors, on the other hand, often self-importantly lecture their audiences, exploring the doom without any productive effort to apply discovered "truths" to practical use for recapturing our destiny. Their pretentious prattling is akin to the display of plumage, clearly revealing a self-serving agenda of self-aggrandizement, visibly relishing every compliment of their intelligence and education.

A community participant, Porridge (Ruination Media2), wrote the following under a Going Free video:

"Your message is simple. We are for White Wellbeing. We are against antiwhitism. This message appeals to everyday people. But this does not appeal to 'thought leaders' because there isn't much to analyze and dissect. It wasn't created by an 18th century French philosopher. It isn't a rabbit hole of alternative worldviews and abstract thinking. If a humble trucker or shelf stacker can learn your methods and put them into practice, that makes the 'thought leaders' redundant. That's why they create intricate webs of abstract ideas which fosters endless pontification and deeper rabbit holes."

An exotic form of content creator that can be found in both of these categories is the **fantasist**. The fantasist documents and dissects doom to stimulate fear, which he or she promises to alleviate with an entrancing solution. These "solutions" are unrealizable. The fantasist's analysis of conditions and prescriptions for remedies are faulty (often intentionally misleading) but intriguing. Such thought leaders are charlatans. Praise, sex and money are their objectives.

In sharp contrast, Going Free is a revolutionary practice and a radical departure from the forms above. In keeping with the Western can-do spirit, Going Free has and continues to serve the objective of recapturing our destiny. We serve that objective by seeking pragmatic solutions to our individual and group challenges, and then subjecting those potential solutions to reason, logic, and evidence as well as the scientific method.

Three Ways You Benefit by Going Free

It's time to take stock of your progress. Name three ways you benefit by Going Free:

Level Two:

Internal Sickness

Welcome to the 2ⁿᵈ Level

of Going Free

I recognize that your decision to Go Free in a society that is unreasonable, hostile, and antiwhite is an act of courage. I congratulate you on the progress you have made thus far.

By this point, you should be able to detect **pervasive antiwhitism** throughout Western Civilization. You can detect the structural unfairness that harms whites for the benefit of nonwhites. The tools provided here will supply you with broader and more profound insights, deepening the awareness and self-actualization you assimilated thus far.

In L1, you learned to turn a critical eye upon society. In L2, you will have to take a hard look in the mirror. Are you ready for a critical look at yourself? Are you ready to be a better you? Are you ready to align with the archetype of *Western Man*? There is still a long way to go, but each step of Going Free brings you closer to achieving your potential-to-power (PTP). The work you do here will create the foundations for perfect health—you will unlock more of your innate physical, mental, and spiritual potential as a Westman.

Before we go any further, it is important for you to understand that antiwhites will dismiss this *curative process*. As with all of their attacks on Westernkind, wherein they *MIS pretext* for their antiwhite jealousy, envy, and hatred, they will MIS pretext to object to Going Free.

An intellectualized argument that antiwhites are likely to use is a phenomenon called the "frequency illusion." The frequency illusion is a cognitive bias wherein anything recently noticed is recurrently noticed. For example, you learn a new word and then see or hear that word several times on subsequent days. The word is not recurring more often than usual. You are merely noticing it. Antiwhites will try to persuade you that MPs are not as frequent as you perceive.

However, your new ability to spot MPs is not an illusion. Rather, it is akin to the training a wilderness guide receives in spotting poisonous snakes amid leaf litter. Once trained, the wilderness guide will spot poisonous snakes as long as he retains his training.

Before choosing to Go Free, you were like other white vagues, unable to spot the camouflaged dangers. Now, like a trained wilderness guide, you can not only protect yourself from poisonous vipers, you can help to guide and train your loved ones and friends.

The Regime will use other tactics to derail your decision to Go Free. They will trivialize and mock Going Free. They will isolate a few MPs, dismissing them without argument, as a product of chance, while stubbornly ignoring the evidence debunking their position. They will cite exceptions to the rule as "proof" there is no rule. They will construct straw man arguments of our positions in order to knock them down. Remember, I foretold it here. The fulfilment of these predictions further validates your decision to Go Free.

Once again, do not look to the Regime, your family or your friends for permission, validation, or approval to Go Free. They are infected with the MPs from which you are Going Free. Their objection to Going Free is evidence that you have made the best decision of your life.

Let's continue.

Keep Your Focus: Going Free

It was necessary to spend time unveiling the Antiwhite Narrative. However, Go Free is not a work of social observation. Rather, the AAP is a tool to help you and our people Go Free from the antiwhite disease—white-noir—undermining your life and our people's destiny.

Internal Threats:

Infections and Symptoms

The Level Two (L2) material is designed to help you identify the MPs you are infected with—as well as establish the causal and exacerbating relationship between those MPs and your white-noir—the spiritual, physical, and emotional trauma that undermines the attainment of your potential and reduces your ability to manifest, attain, and satisfy your desires.

The most destructive MPs are locked deeply in the subconscious mind, making them difficult to identify and address. The process of identifying the causal and exacerbating links between MPs and your white-noir is complicated by a host of factors, such as the dynamism of human thought and the circumstance, variation, and date of infection.

For example, the earlier in life you were infected with an MP, the greater the control it wields over your thoughts and behavior. The most powerful MP infections, therefore, are those we are infected with as children.

Once you identify the MPs you are infected with, you will be able to examine them objectively: Why do you hold these superstitions? Who taught you these harmful beliefs and attitudes? Who were the original purveyors and what was their intent?

Finally, by developing these skillsets, your elevation will allow you to receive further instruction for Going Free, enabling you to climb higher toward your full mental, physical, and spiritual potential as a member of Westernkind.

Your Potential-to-Power:

MPs, White-Noir, and Bio-Spirit

MP infection reduces your **potential-to-power (PTP)**. In the simplest terms, your PTP is your ability to attain what you want. More fully, your PTP is the aggregate of your bio-spiritual potential to manifest, attain, and satisfy your desires. The boundaries of your personal abilities are defined by both internal and external factors. Internally, it is your unique bio-spiritual architecture that establishes the limits of your potential.

However, your natural potential can be limited by external forces. These external forces—specifically MPs and our antiwhite environment—undermine your natural ability to manifest, attain, and satisfy your desires.

The consequence of MP infection is white-noir. We suffer white-noir as individuals, and as a people. White-noir is the sum of the spiritual, psychological, and physiological abnormalities that undermine your PTP.

In essence, you are an eagle who has had its wings fettered to its sides since hatching. You have been made to trudge through the dust with flightless birds, and you haven't the slightest notion that you could soar amid the heavens.

But Going Free breaks your fetters. Your white-noir is in the muscles and joints of your wings, weak and frail from disuse. It is also in your mind—the mental barriers that prevent you from realizing your destiny in the heights.

Medical science and common sense tell us that destructive beliefs and attitudes (every MP is destructive for whites) retard and undermine a person's health, abilities, drive, and resiliency. Such people are at a marked disadvantage in every endeavor.

Let's think back to the story of Buddy Smith. Buddy was infected with the "anti-Smith MPs." He saw himself as dumb and his choices and life skills reflected this. Buddy didn't know that so much of his potential was undermined by his "Smith-noir."

Likewise, Westmen who are not aware of their white-noir are oblivious to these abnormalities limiting their PTP and undermining their health.

To make matters worse, we live our lives in environments that are increasingly uncomfortable, alien, and hostile to us. Recall our discussion of the bio-spirit. In simplified terms, a people's bio-spirit can be thought of as their distinct biological instincts.

Each people project their instincts onto their environment. The sum of these projections is the people's culture. The *cultural reflection* of a person's *instinctual projection* induces feelings of peace, stability, permanence, harmony. The opposite is true for a person in an environment that does not reflect their bio-spirit.

The more we are white-guilted into altering our communities to suit the bio-spirits (instincts) of nonwhites, the less our communities reflect *our own* bio-spiritual nature. The less our communities reflect our bio-spirit, the more unfamiliar, unstable, and uncomfortable these communities feel—exacerbating our white-noir.

Oblivious to the white-noir limiting your PTP and undermining your health, you are habituated and resigned to humiliation, mediocrity, failure, and disappointment in all areas of life: problem solving, coping skills, interpersonal interaction, education, work, romance, parenting, etc.

To reap the full benefits of Going Free, you must immerse yourself in the AAP—and Go Free. Doing so will reduce the damaging effects of stress, which can:

- Improve your health.

- Enhance your memory.

- Unleash your intelligence.

- Stimulate your creativity.

- Develop your relationships.

- Magnify your productivity.

- Elevate your mood.

- Enable you to take charge of your life.

- Align with the archetype of Western Man.

- On a global scale, Going Free will restore tranquility, order, and safety to Western Civilization by restoring physical, mental, and spiritual harmony to Westernkind.

Your Examples of Nonwhite Bio-Spiritual Projections
in Your Community or a Community You Visited

In your own words, give three examples of nonwhite bio-spiritual projections (instinct) in your community (or a community you visited) that make you feel uncomfortable, out of place, or fearful, such as nonwhite behavior, customs, architectural design or dress, holiday decorations, etc.:

The Effects on White Children

You may feel embarrassed to realize we have been tricked into acting in ways harmful to ourselves, our countries, and our people. As adults, we like to think of ourselves as tough, independent, and resistant to manipulation.

Recall again the vignettes about the children Buddy Smith, Tommy, and Lilly. A white child's view of himself, his kind, and every other group of people is taught to him—*imposed* on him—by antiwhites. This antiwhite worldview is a crippling and disfiguring power which compromises the physical, mental, and spiritual health of all white children.

The timing of this abusive indoctrination is particularly destructive because the minds of white children are still forming—making children the most vulnerable to the devastating effects of antiwhitism. The lies and manipulations of antiwhitism disfigure their thought processes and their deductive and logical reasoning abilities. Their white-noir can present as any number of physical diseases and psychiatric disorders.

When I write of white children, I mean *all* white children. No child escapes MP infection—no matter the child or their upbringing. You may think that you are an exception because of your conservative or religious upbringing. Sadly, you are wrong. No child escapes the abuse of antiwhitism and MPs in modernity. A white positive woman named Mary illustrates this fact.

Mary firmly believed that she was infected with only five MPs. She claimed that her parents had been *"very conservative"* and had dutifully disabused her of many antiwhite superstitions during her childhood. The suggestion that she might be extensively infected offended Mary—it felt to her like an attack on her parents for failing to protect her, as well as an insult to her intelligence.

To Mary's credit, she eventually acknowledged that we have all been deeply deceived. She accepted that her parents couldn't have protected her from everything. She realized her intelligence could not have protected her in her childhood, because as children we are innocent and trusting.

Moreover, childhood is a time when the mental tools we use to understand the world are still forming. That acceptance and vulnerability enabled her to truly begin Going Free. Though horrified by the scope of her condition, Mary tripled her efforts to Go Free and was mightily rewarded. Just as an undiagnosed cancer cannot be treated, undiagnosed MPs cannot be identified and neutralized.

Antiwhitism engenders thoughts that penetrate deeply into the subconscious, infecting the minds of white children with inescapably illogical deductions that damage their health. These infections set the stage for short and long-term disease and psychiatric disorders.

Such illogical deductions encourage bad and irrational decision-making in white children in every area of their lives: personal interaction, education, drug use, sexuality, recklessness, betrayal of and fanatical opposition to Westernkind, etc.

Have you seen or suspected such factors in your own or someone else's life? Might your displeasure with your body or appearance be attributable to antiwhite notions? Could your friend's drug addiction or suicide have its root in a hopelessness engendered by antiwhitism? Could your unemployment or lack of promotion be a consequence of antiwhite beliefs in yourself and others?

Uncovering Your MPs

It takes both courage and humility to identify and neutralize the MPs you are infected with. Introspection can be difficult. We must learn to see ourselves as we truly are, rather than as we would like to be. This forces us to face parts of ourselves that we would rather not face. We must be brave enough for self-criticism, and humble enough to acknowledge that we have been bamboozled.

Diagnosing our MP infection can be made more difficult because it is possible to mask our symptoms. For example, if you are infected with the MP that *"Westmen are more destructive of the environment than other races,"* you may attempt to suppress this by speaking about all the good that Westmen and Western countries do for the planet.

Such behavior is akin to medications which provide *symptomatic relief.* Just as suppressing the outward symptoms of a cold does not cure one's cold, efforts to suppress the symptoms of MPs are not the same as Going Free.

Let's explore the MPs you are infected with. Contemplate how many times during your reading of L1 you saw yourself in the examples and were shocked to find your own subconscious assumptions matching up with MPs, or your own experience revealed in antiwhitism.

Most people can identify three or four of the MPs with which they are infected. Those who are more perceptive will identify more. The following examples of MPs are merely intended to get you thinking about which MPs you are infected with. Reflect on whether you have ever claimed, suspected, or agreed with any of the following MPs.

- *"Whites are awkward and clumsy."*
- *"Blondes are dumb."*
- *"Whites often succeed in educational, social, and professional settings because they unfairly support one another at the expense of nonwhites."*
- *"Whites are more likely to be intolerant of those not like themselves, whereas nonwhites are more likely to be welcoming."*
- *"Whites are responsible for slavery."*
- *"White people have waged more wars, or waged them more cruelly, than nonwhites."*

- *"White people are inherently disposed to persecuting and exploiting others."*
- *"Whites are more callous and less sympathetic than nonwhites."*

The MPs with which we have been infected from childhood are so *deeply rooted in the fabric of who we are* that they become indistinguishable from our individual identities. Our ongoing studies reveal that the average Westman is infected with five to thirty times the MPs that he personally diagnoses.

Another way to diagnose your MP infections is to consider if your feelings are reflective of MP infection.

- Have you ever felt the need to apologize for being white—to itemize all the reasons that whites should feel guilty, or to quote nonwhites on white "villainy" in hopes of receiving social acceptance and respect?
- Have you ever felt afraid to complain about the antiwhite double standards in society because you might be denounced as a "bigot?"
- Have you ever wondered whether it was wrong of you to suspect race as a factor when you were passed over for hiring or promotion in favor of a nonwhite?

- Have you ever felt rootless? Have you ever felt like you have no culture—no people? Have you ever felt lost as a result? Has your life seemed purposeless as a consequence?

- Has society's lack of concern for you and our people made you feel like life is not worth living?

- Has society's narrative that you and our people are born guilty and responsible for suffering in the world ever led you to contemplate the ultimate white flight of suicide because the world would be better off without you, an "evil" white person?

- Do you perceive yourself as lacking because white people are uninteresting or less "cool" than nonwhites?

- Have you asked yourself whether someone you wished to ask on a date would prefer a nonwhite?

- Do you feel that you need to darken your skin ("get a tan") in order to be attractive? Do you believe you need fleshier lips, protruding buttocks, or a smaller head to be attractive? Is it possible your dissatisfaction with your appearance is due to an antiwhite expectation of beauty, where nonwhite features and skin tones are considered the new beautiful?

- Did you embrace nonwhite culture and date nonwhites, rejecting everything white and Western? Have you asked yourself what role the MPs that everything white and Western is villainous (whereas everything nonwhite is virtuous) played in your decision?

What spiritual injury do you think you did to yourself by rejecting our people and yourself? Destructive beliefs and attitudes (such as antiwhite MPs) retard and undermine a person's spirit, health, abilities, drive, and resiliency, instigating numerous and cascading abnormalities. Have you ever asked yourself what it means to be taught—from your earliest childhood—that you are a member of a guilty people—a people that has a long history of harming the innocent around the world?

- Have you ever considered the stress-inducing element of seeing other groups receive preferential treatment and privileges, while you and your people are defined as common and unimportant?
- How deeply has it hurt you to know that your experiences (as far as the Regime is concerned) don't matter, that whether or not you succeed in life doesn't matter, that whether or not you suffer or have joy

doesn't matter—*because you're white*? How deeply does it hurt you to know that only the experiences of nonwhites matter—that only nonwhite success, suffering, and joy matter?

- What experiences, joy, and rewards did you miss out on because you were struggling to get your bearings, rather than forging ahead to the fulfilment of your dreams?

MPs have caused or exacerbated every single problem in your life. They warp our understanding of the world. MPs confuse our decision-making processes and deform our characters.

As referenced earlier, like an eagle whose fate calls it to the sky, but whose wings, fettered to its sides, confine it to the ground, our spirit wants to spread its wings and rise to new heights. But a distorted view of ourselves and the world confines us to a life of mediocrity, bad decisions, unrealized potential and even physical illness.

Going Free can improve your condition whether or not you initially identify the specific MPs from which you are suffering. But full recovery and empowerment often requires identifying all MPs and treating them on an ongoing basis.

Do You Speak or Write Like an Antiwhite?

Do you ever notice yourself or others speaking or writing from the antiwhite perspective when objecting to antiwhitism?

1. *"We are the bad ones, so we are supposed to shut up and do what we are told."*

2. *"They want their diverse, rainbow utopia where everyone is happy."*

3. *"We are supposed to help the migrants and prove that we are good people."*

4. *"I want to preserve my traditions, and that makes me evil."*

5. *"They are stunningly brave heroes when they radically change our societies."*

6. *"We are the good guys if we reject those bad white people who care about Western Civilization."*

Speaking or writing from the antiwhite perspective is indicative of deep psychological wounds—of white–noir. Such behavior is an attempt to "medicate" white-noir with a passive aggressive irreverence toward antiwhitism and the **antiwhite oligarchs**. Very often, those "medicating" their white-noir in this fashion will articulate many of the MPs with which they are infected.

In the examples the speaker or writer mentioned numerous MPs:

1. Whites are the "bad guys."
2. Multiracialism is a "positive" and leads to "greater benefits."
3. Westmen are "moral" if they empower nonwhites at the expense of whites.
4. Serving White Wellbeing is "immoral."
5. Antiwhites are our "betters."
6. Opposing White Wellbeing is "moral" and makes one a "good" person.

Whether you or others have spoken or written like an antiwhite, use these opportunities to identify MPs in yourself. And make a commitment to yourself that you will never—or never again—speak or write like an antiwhite.

Which MPs are You Infected With?

In your own words, give three examples of MPs you are infected with:

MPs and Your White-Noir

In your own words, give three examples of MPs you are infected with and the potential (causative or exacerbating) connections to your diseases, character flaws, or destructive decisions you've made in your life:

Your Growth Since Beginning to Go Free

Some Westmen report a slowly expanding improvement in their clarity of thought and perception when they begin Going Free. Others recount explosive epiphanies, making them feel as though they have never truly seen the world.

Some feel an overwhelming desire to plow deeper. Others may just feel overwhelmed. Whatever your experience, it is perfectly valid and part of the healing process. Name three changes you have noticed in yourself since you began Going Free:

Level Three:

Treatment

Welcome to the 3rd Level

of Going Free

Congratulations! You have come a long way. By this point, you may be troubled by how many of those around you remain trapped in ignorance, delusion, and even hostility toward Westmen Going Free.

It can be difficult to continue with the process when you think about the vast number who remain infected. It can feel like a lonely journey. But you are not alone. More people than you realize are Going Free. There is a **Great White Awakening** happening now! As more and more of our people are Going Free there is an exponential momentum.

The Great White Awakening has produced milestones in the freeing of our people that signify an increasing impossibility of arresting the momentum of our cause! You are part of this heroic journey for our people.

Your new awareness peels back the malicious façade that has kept you entangled in antiwhite delusions. You have established the basis for self-actualization. You should now be able to detect pervasive antiwhitism and the injustices that grow therefrom—harming whites for the benefit of antiwhites.

Again, I challenge you to rededicate and redouble your efforts to Go Free. Are you ready to answer the difficult questions? Are you ready to take a hard look in the mirror? Are you ready to be a better you? Are you ready to align with the archetype of Western Man?

There is still a long way to go, but each step of Going Free brings you closer to achieving your PTP. Your work is creating the foundations for perfect health, and accessing your true physical, mental and spiritual potential as a Westman.

Once again, do not look to the Regime, your friends or family for permission, validation, or approval to Go Free. They are infected with the MPs from which you are Going Free. Their objection to Going Free is proof that you have made the best decision of your life.

Let's continue.

Self-Generated Opposition:

Healing and Renewal

In L3, you will be introduced to the methods for *treating* MP infections and for *immunizing* yourself against further infections. You will develop the important skillsets that derive from the dialectics and lexicon of Going Free. You will learn how to address MPs as you encounter or sense them within yourself, treating them and weakening them as you grow stronger. You will learn how to address and immunize yourself against new MPs as they present themselves in your environment. You will be empowered by productive **thought chains**, developing behaviors that will erode the foundations by which MPs easily infect and sway you.

Finally, by developing these skillsets, your elevation will allow you to receive further instruction for Going Free— enabling you to climb higher toward your innate mental, physical, and spiritual potential.

Identify—Treat—Go Free:

Your Subconscious Mind

Recall our discussion of the role of the subconscious mind and the power of the subconscious mind to (largely) govern our lives. It makes thousands of learned decisions/judgments instantly and without recourse to our conscious minds. For example, it enabled our remote ancestors to pick and eat berries, while the conscious mind remained alert to threats and opportunities. Today, among many other activities, it enables us to drive our cars while we use our conscious minds for other matters, such as thinking about what we have to do later in the day. Obviously, the power of the subconscious to inform and guide us is of great benefit to us.

However, it can also be an Achilles heel. The subconscious mind is like a block of clay that can be molded—without our intent or recognition, and irrespective of reason, logic, and evidence.

It indiscriminately absorbs information, regardless of truth or falsehood. People whose minds are untrained are easily convinced of falsehoods. If such falsehoods are not dispelled, they seat themselves firmly in our subconscious minds. The longer they go unchallenged, the deeper they are buried. Importantly, this increasing depth *conceals and strengthens* their influence over our identities.

Such deep infections are so thoroughly ingrained in the origin of our personalities and characters that it is difficult to differentiate them from ourselves. Consider emotionally-charged beliefs, such as religion or politics. It can be difficult to differentiate such beliefs from ourselves. If we try to imagine ourselves without such beliefs, the person we imagine may no longer seem like *us*. In other words, such beliefs come to form part of our *identity*.

Tragically, this same process has occurred with MPs in Westernkind.

The MPs which we have been infected with were delivered as factual, authoritative, and sacred by the many arms of the Regime—the governments, academia, and news and entertainment media. Furthermore, social authorities have reinforced these ideas throughout our lives by rewarding those who conform, and punishing those who dissent.

Our subconscious minds, as a result of this formative-period molding and lifelong reinforcement, are deeply infected with a broad range of MPs.

Conscious and unconscious thoughts are similar to surface and deep-sea currents. Surface currents, like conscious thoughts, are superficial relative to deep-sea currents/subconscious thoughts. Deep-sea currents drive the oceans around our planet. Whereas surface currents can be altered by the wind, the deep-sea currents are the pulse and governing power in the ocean. Interestingly, we use the saying *"wherever the wind blows"* to underscore the ease with which conscious opinion changes.

But these surface, superficial opinions and currents that are easily changed are much less important to you, your identity, and your process of Going Free. Rather, it is the deep-sea currents, the MPs infecting your subconscious, which you need to address to truly Go Free.

Triggers in Your Subconscious

Cues from your environment and your conscious thoughts *trigger* MPs in your subconscious mind.

A cue is any element in your environment or conscious thoughts that activates an MP you are infected with. For example, you are standing at a bus stop with a group of strangers. A white man gives each of you a leaflet that warns about nonwhite violence and the dangers of a growing antiwhite nonwhite population. While riding on the bus, you wonder if your family will be safe in a community composed increasingly of other peoples.

The leaflet is an external cue; the thought you had while on the bus was an internal cue. Both activated MPs with which you are infected. Once an MP has been triggered, the interpretive mandates connected to each antiwhite precept are evoked by your subconscious. For example, you likely feel shame or that you are "doing something wrong" for holding or even listening to or reading opinions that conflict with antiwhitism. You feel like an outcast, ugly, uneducated, frightened, etc.

Imagine that you stand on a small stage, surrounded by a random crowd of strangers. A man on a megaphone tells the group that you don't think the races are identical; that you reject diversity; that you prefer associating with your own people. All eyes are on you—how do you feel?

By contrast, when you endorse antiwhitism you feel righteous. You feel welcomed, supported, intelligent, virtuous. Same stage—same crowd—same man on a megaphone telling the crowd that you think everyone is identical; that you support diversifying your workplace or school; that you enjoy your contact with exotic cultures.

These thoughts and feelings are automatic and instantaneous. By the time you begin consciously examining the cues that triggered these thoughts and feelings, you have *already* interpreted, judged, and measured the cues by antiwhite "standards" of right and wrong.

You have already considered the cues at the speed of subconscious thoughts—which is to conscious thought as the speed of a jet fighter to a biplane. Even if you consciously know that the antiwhite interpretations, judgments, and measurements are wrong, your conscious mind is forced to wrestle with your subconscious for the prize of your identity.

What's worse, not only have your conscious thoughts arrived late to the struggle, but you are further disadvantaged because your conscious mind requires effort to wage the fight—your subconscious mind does not.

Confront, Challenge, Dispel

To combat white-noir and mitigate the control MPs exercise over your thoughts and behavior, you must use your conscious mind to override your subconscious mind. You must **Confront, Challenge, and Dispel (CCD)** your MPs the instant they are triggered. You do this by consciously **counter asserting** with MCs.

We CCD because MPs cannot be erased from our subconscious minds. There is no mechanism whereby we can simply delete these ingrained infections. However, by consistently *CCDing*, you build **counter triggers**.

These counter triggers eventually become part of your subconscious mind. When an MP is triggered by a cue in your environment or your conscious thoughts, your counter trigger is triggered by the MP, thereby decreasing (and even negating) the MP's influence.

Cue => triggered MP => triggered counter trigger =>
MP negated

Establishing subconscious counter triggers is fundamental to the process of Going Free.

To CCD, you must create a *countervailing statement* (a statement that offsets the MP with equal or greater force) as opposed to a disapproving statement. For example, if confronted with the MP that *"diversity is strength,"* it would be incorrect to say, *"Diversity isn't strength"* or *"It's not true that diversity is strength."*

Rather, when confronted with the MP that *"diversity is strength,"* CCD with one or more of the following: *"Diversity is weakness—diversity is conflict—diversity is discomfort—diversity is white erasure—diversity is dis-synergistic—diversity is death."*

Let us consider another MP and how to CCD when it is triggered. A foundational MP (that many other MPs are built upon) is *"Westernkind is uniquely responsible for slavery."* When you encounter this MP in your environment (a plot point in a novel, newspaper story, television show, movie trailer, etc.) or in your thoughts (reflecting on what you had learned about slavery at school) you must CCD.

Remind yourself that Westernkind did not invent slavery. Slavery has been practiced around the world since prehistoric times.

Every race has enslaved every other race. Recall that the nonwhite peoples of the world have Westernkind to thank for the time, treasure, and lives we sacrificed to put an end to slavery during the 19th century to achieve our ideal of a world without slavery.

Remember to tell yourself that antiwhites want to infect and white-guilt us with these MPs to harm our people and enrich themselves at our expense.

Here is another example of an MP infection. The sight of a shabby nonwhite neighborhood may trigger the thought that its inhabitants live in squalor and violence because our people have "disadvantaged" them. Again, you must counter assert.

Remind yourself that Westernkind is not responsible for the neighborhood's condition. Westernkind did not cause its inhabitants to be less intelligent or do less planning for the future. Nonwhites have agency, and must live with the consequences of their decisions and behavior—just like Westmen. Remind yourself that antiwhites want to infect us with white-guilt in order to turn us against our own people.

Remind yourself—in every case—that the antiwhite ideas, concepts, feelings, etc. that well up within you are the "smoking gun" evidence of the crimes antiwhites have committed against you, everyone you love, and our people. Use the righteous anger you generate from these moments to vigorously combat that part of yourself that remains infected, that continues to do the bidding of your victimizers long after they infected you.

Make a commitment to never sacrifice our people so that you can socially signal that you are a "good" person by antiwhite "standards." Make a commitment to yourself to remember that all of these "good" feelings are an illusion. These "good" feelings are actually further injuring you and our people—and specifically our children.

Your Examples of CCDing MP Infections

In your own words, formulate a CCD statement you could make in response to the MP that *"Westmen create social conditions which compel nonwhites to deal drugs."*

Remember to create a countervailing statement (a statement that offsets the MP with equal or greater force) as opposed to a disapproving statement. Focus at least one of your answers on the fact that antiwhites want to infect and white-guilt us with MPs to suppress your well-being and our efforts to secure the well-being of our people and children:

Meme-Curatives (MCs)

Meme-curatives (MCs) are the remedies for MPs. MCs are tools that work like MPs, but rather than harm you they empower you. I have coined many powerful MCs and below I share some of these and others. See Appendices for an expanded list of MPs and MCs.

- *"It is not the similarities that make us the same; it is the differences that make us different."* This is an extremely powerful MC. I have successfully used it hundreds if not thousands of times to defeat MPs in myself and others. This MC is so powerful because it defeats the MP *"All races of man are the same,"* on which so much of antiwhitism is built.

- *"Racial differences are not skin-deep. They extend to the essence of our being."* Antiwhites often trivialize the profound racial differences by saying the difference among the races is no more than pigment or skin tone.

- **Forced multiracial harmonizing**: We are forced to harmonize the racial diversity, which massively diverts our resources, time, talent and money. And that massive consumption of our resources radically lowers our quality of life in all areas of our lives.

- *"Mutual discomfort as a consequence of bio-spiritual incompatibility is the basis of governmental tyranny and violent balkanization."* governments employ escalating intrusions on privacy and punishments to keep the mutually antagonistic peoples at "peace."

- **Antiwhite slurs**: The language of white oppression/white erasure: Words like "racist," "bigot," "anti-Semite," "hater," "xenophobe," "homophobe," "sexist," "fascist," etc. While certain antiwhite slurs may have reasonable definitions in some contexts, they are all inextricably bound to MPs in the average person's mind. As a practitioner of Going Free, you should strive to avoid using antiwhite slurs in any context, as their usage reinforces and legitimizes antiwhitism. They inflict harm on Westernkind by demonizing us and preventing us from defending ourselves. Antiwhite slurs offend you.

- *"There is no excellence where there is equality. Eventually, there isn't even competence."* There is no competence or excellence because everyone is reduced to the least capable or able to achieve "equality," which is largely defined as "outcome of *result*" rather than *opportunity*. Increasingly, however, antiwhites use "equity" in the place of "equality," which is largely defined as "equality" by way of superior outcome for nonwhites.

- **Numerical diffidence**: The state in which a people, within the body of another people or peoples, is reluctant to project their bio-spirit onto their environment for fear of upsetting/angering the other people or peoples. Prior to achieving numerical courage, nonwhites in Western countries are in a state of numerical diffidence. While in this state, nonwhites superficially conform to the bio-spiritual expression of Westernkind.

- **Numerical courage**: The state in which a people, within the body of another people or peoples, confidently projects their bio-spirit onto their environment without concern for the other people or peoples. The point at which nonwhites within Western countries manifest and project their bio-spiritual expressions (which are at variance with white expression) onto Western Civilization. This process initiates a cultural arms race which always ends in oppressive governmental tyranny and violent balkanization.

- **<u>Virtue trapping</u>**: Typically a tactic employed by antiwhites, virtue trapping is when an advocate for White Wellbeing is criticized for not "perfectly" exemplifying a virtue that he or we maintain as necessary for a healthy life and community. When confronted by this tactic, defeat it by naming the tactic and identifying what he is doing.

- Multiracialism: Do not use the word "multiculturalism," and correct the use in others Going Free.

- *"Diversity is dis-synergistic—multiracialism is dis-synergistic."* We are less than the sum of our parts.

- *"If you abide by antiwhitism, you reinforce antiwhitism."* Thoughts and behaviors that conform to antiwhitism strengthen antiwhitism.

- *"Maturing socio-politically."* By Going Free, you are maturing socio-politically. All those who move toward White Wellbeing—from one socio-political concept to the next—are maturing socio-politically. By helping others to Go Free, we are helping them to mature socio-politically.

- Victimizer: The antiwhites are our victimizers. Try not to use the word "enemy" for antiwhites because "enemy" implies some measure of equal ability and desire to inflict harm, which we do not possess. I speak at greater length on this in the chapter *Know Your Enemy (Not Enemies)* below.

- *"We are the Elect of our people."* All Westmen who care about our people and our creations are the best of their families, communities, states, and countries. All of these people who also Go Free are the best of the best—the Elect of Westernkind.

- *"We are white positive/we are Wellbeing advocates."* Those who disagree with White Wellbeing are antiwhite. As antiwhitism harms everyone and everything, antiwhites are the enemy of humanity and the planet. We, as practitioners of Going Free, champion humanity and nature.

- **Pristine**: Places/people/states of mind/things inside Western societies that are largely untainted by antiwhitism and unaffected by white erasure, having *remained in* or possibly *returned to* the "pristine" state they historically were in.

- **Curative contagion**: The AAP—Going Free.

- *"Anger/defense/etc. is a virtue when it protects the innocent."* Often, antiwhites undermine Wellbeing advocates by using reverse psychologically. They accuse you of being "angry," "hateful" or "fearful," and they explicitly or implicitly offer to withdraw the accusation if you embrace antiwhitism. Rather than fall for their trap, respond by stating that anger is a virtue when it protects the innocent. When they say that you are afraid or hateful of a degenerate lifestyle, or that you are afraid or hateful of nonwhite immigrants, you say that you are a *defender* of White Wellbeing, and that *defense is a virtue when it protects the innocent.*

- Equivalence Fallacy: This is when antiwhites draw tenuous or false equivalencies. For example, citing the good behavior of nonwhite individuals to draw a false equivalence between the bio-spiritual harmony (high-trust/high social engagement/etc.) of homogenous Western Civilization and the bio-spiritual incompatibility of multiracial societies that white-erase Westernkind: you feel the bio-spiritual disharmony (alienated in your own community) discomfort, and increasing physical threat of being the last white person in your community, but at least your neighbor mows his yard. Name and identify what the antiwhite is doing to defeat this tactic.

- *"Increasing my likelihood of dying from X is not legitimized by saying that I am already likely to die from Y."* For example, antiwhites will say that we already might get raped by a white rapist, so why object to bringing nonwhite rapists into the country. Or, antiwhites will say that we already might get murdered by a white murderer, so why object to increasing the likelihood of being murdered by a nonwhite terrorist.

- *"Diversity is white erasure."* So-called "diversity" is an attack on Westmen because it means fewer white people.

- Diversity hire/fire (or diversity selection/rejection): We focus on the consequences for our people rather than the special treatment for nonwhites or other "victim" groups. For every diversity hire, there is a diversity fire; for every diversity selection, there is a diversity rejection: jobs, promotions, raises, enrollment, and government contracting, etc. As there are a finite number of these things, and as whites are the only group that can be legally and socially discriminated against, earmarking by race and official "victim" group automatically victimizes a white person.

- *"Equality is the demand of the incompetent to handicap the competent."* Further, it is the argument the privileged use to "justify" robbing those whom they misname "privileged." Framing demands as "equality" is an attempt to stand on "the moral high ground" in order to conceal the self-serving nature of the demand.

- **Heresy**: When you are victimized by antiwhites for holding opinions heretical to antiwhitism—when you are not antiwhite or antiwhite enough. Do not say that this or that white person was fired or jailed for X (insert the antiwhite charge here, such as "racism" or hurtful speech). Antiwhites are not protecting nonwhites. They are victimizing you for heresy to antiwhitism because you are not antiwhite enough.

- **Social lynching**: This is when friends, family, and strangers react negatively and often collectively to victimize Westmen who heretically deviate from antiwhitism. Social lynching often begins with antiwhite slurs and ends in ostracism and character and career assassination. The verbal framework of

Going Free wards against social lynching, as well as providing appropriate responses to it.

- **Antiwhite tribunal**: Any antiwhite or group of antiwhites that sit in judgment, meting punishment for heresy to antiwhitism.

- **White erasure**: When to the detriment of White Wellbeing: The removal, rewriting, renaming, defacing, expunging, etc. of anything related to or of Westernkind.

- **Hate hoax**: Any covert act—committed by one or more antiwhites in the guise of a white person or people—that conforms to the Antiwhite Narrative and thereby demonizes Westmen is a hate hoax. Hate hoaxes draw the noose of suspicion around the throats of all white people, and thereby are "hate crimes" against our entire race. Such crimes are used to "justify" past, present, and future harm to Westernkind, from violent attacks on white men, women and children by antiwhite individuals in the name of imagined "revenge," to discriminatory antiwhite policies at the institutional level.

- **Hush crime**: All acts that victimize one or more Westmen, and by so doing contradict and/or disprove the Antiwhite Narrative, and are therefore obfuscated, lied about, downplayed, ignored, or given comparatively little publicity/attention by antiwhites. Not all hush crimes are "criminal"; some are legal but socially condemned acts. Debunked hate hoaxes routinely become hush crimes. Hush crime is a powerful MC because the premise reveals the truth about antiwhite domination of Regime news and entertainment media.

- All words and phrases that I have created or adopted to serve Going Free are MCs, such as **MIS**, **MP**, **Westernkind**, **Westman**, **Westmen**, **White Wellbeing**, **bio-spirit**, etc.

Finally, the two most powerful MCs: The first is a universal response that can be successfully used against any antiwhite argument, and the second—**Antiwhite Screed**—is the key to unlock, understand and predict antiwhite speech and actions.

Universal Response

MC: *"No matter what you say, if your conclusion is antiwhite I reject it!"*

The Antiwhite Screed

Antiwhite speech and actions are difficult to understand for those unfamiliar with antiwhite motivations (as outlined in "The Path to Becoming an Antiwhite" in this book).

The MC below encapsulates antiwhite motives in a way that will help you understand and predict antiwhite speech and actions:

To understand and predict antiwhite speech and deed, simply apply the Antiwhite Screed:

(*Ceteris paribus*, or excluding unusual circumstances:) *"Everything conducive to White Wellbeing is negative. Conversely, everything antithetic to White Wellbeing is positive."*

Regularly applying this MC is an essential step in the process of Going Free.

Practice Your Newfound Skills

As is the case in all human endeavors, practice makes perfect. Indeed, the adage that *"if we are not marching forward, we are falling backward"* is nowhere truer than in practicing the new skills of MP identification and CCDing.

There are many ways that you can practice these skillsets that are engaging and illuminating. For example, a favorite of Roi Danton, a dedicated participant in the White Wellbeing community, is to revisit old songs, movies, games, books and television shows.

When you revisit such material, do not passively read, listen, or watch. Rather, sit on the edge of your seat. Watch, listen, or read for five-to fifteen-minute increments. The goal here is to *stay consciously focused* on examining the material for the presence of MPs. And most importantly, use a computer, tablet, phone, or pen and pad to jot down the MPs as you identify them.

This is a powerful exercise for building the "muscles" you need to identify MPs, and it is essential exercise to develop the ability to identify new MPs as you are exposed to them; however, do not revisit such material until you truly understand what to look for.

Many find this practice to be shocking, even infuriating, so prepare yourself for the disorientation you will experience. Discovering that comfortable and even happy memories from your life are fraught with MPs that were poisoning you and undermining your PTP can engender resentment, anger and sadness. Even a sense of loss is not uncommon and is all part of the healing process.

Finally, share your discoveries with others, such as your **Going Free friend (GFF)**. Teaching them about your discoveries will deepen and magnify your efforts.

An additional exercise is to *translate* all antiwhite material you read or hear. Do this whether it is just for yourself or sharing with others. For example, an article in a newspaper may read, *"White Supremacists Protest Censorship."* Translate this as *"Heretics to Antiwhitism Protest Censorship."* A news reader on TV who says, *"Right-wing radicals gather in park to protect statue,"* should be translated by you: *"He means that 'Heroes gather in park to protect statue.'"*

Translating is a vital practice, especially when translating for children, as it strengthens your MP identification and MC creation, as well as your awareness of our identity, the objectives and tactics of antiwhites, and their seats in positions of power.

Know Your Enemy

(Not Enemies)

We, as white men and women, do not have enemies; we have a single victimizer.

What group of people is our victimizer? *Antiwhites*.

Do not needlessly divide those who victimize us into a nuanced laundry list of victimizers. Do not call them by the names of their taking: Marxists, cultural Marxists, economic Marxists, liberals, globalists, progressives, feminists (first wave, second wave, third wave), Chicano nationalists, black nationalists, neocons, social justice warriors and so on—they all become *antiwhites* whenever they cause, seek or support the harm of Westernkind.

By giving them the names of their taking, you *empower* them and *disempower* us.

By identifying them with the names of their taking, you put yourself in their story rather than forcing them into ours.

By focusing on antiwhite groups individually, you put the emphasis in the wrong place, depriving us of the perspective that stimulates ideas to protect ourselves from all antiwhites—both big and small. *Love for our people unites us—not anger for another group.*

By dividing them into many categories, you create the illusion that we are outnumbered—you cause fear—you stimulate doubt and second-guessing, and thereby you deprive yourself and us of the righteous indignation we need to defend ourselves.

By dividing them into many categories, you miss the thread that binds them—the only thread that matters for our and therefore your well-being—that they are all antiwhite. Distinct antiwhite groups always overlook their mutually exclusive doctrines in order to act in concert against us.

Even with incompatible ideologies, antiwhites are able to unite because they have a common victim (Westmen) that they underhandedly name "oppressor." Having an "oppressor" gives them the right of self-defense, which creates the illusion that they are united as they inflict harm on us and our civilization.

When you must identify a specific group of antiwhites for clarity, return to referring to them as "antiwhites" as soon as possible. Moreover, do not say "white antiwhites," "black antiwhites," or "Jewish antiwhites," etc. unless clarity requires it. And again, return to "antiwhite" as soon as possible—*because that is all that truly matters.*

Finally, do not use the word enemy unless you have to. Use the words "victimizer" and "victimizers" for antiwhites. Antiwhites are our victimizers.

The word enemy implies some measure of equality in the injury that the individuals or groups can and do inflict on each other. There is no equality of injury between Westernkind (specifically those serving White Wellbeing) and antiwhites. At present, we are more like a chained captive, tormented and tortured by a sadistic abductor. Antiwhites are our victimizers: Our *victimizers* demonize us in the media. Our *victimizers* prevent us from holding meetings. Our *victimizers* censor us from social media and payment processing platforms.

Antiwhites are our victimizers. Use it.

The Elect,

The Vague

and

The Victimizer

The antiwhite chooses to be antiwhite; we do not make that decision for him. We merely recognize the choice.

No person or group of people is antiwhite by way of immutable characteristics, such as race and sex. Rather, choosing to think antiwhite thoughts, act in antiwhite ways, or participate in antiwhite ideologies or strategies makes one antiwhite.

As Wellbeing advocates, we recognize the choices people make relative to our well-being. People who choose to serve White Wellbeing are the *Elect*. Those who choose to be antiwhite are *victimizers*. And everyone who has not made a choice relative to White Wellbeing is a *vague*.

Antiwhites Are Not Hypocrites

Seeing antiwhite hypocrisy is one of the first steps to Going Free, but the path to true understanding is only opened when you realize that *there is no hypocrisy.*

Antiwhite behavior only appears hypocritical when you incorrectly accept antiwhite pretexts as the honest reasons for their behaviors. For example, white conservatives are fond of using nonwhite conservatives to espouse conservative positions.

White conservatives believe the antiwhite pretext that *"nonwhites and their opinions are especially important and deserve to be yielded or deferred to"* because of MPs such as *"historical oppression," "legacy of slavery," "structural racism"* and the like.

White conservatives shake their heads and condemn the "hypocrisy" when antiwhites slander nonwhite conservatives with the same antiwhite slurs that are used against white conservatives, such as "racist," "bigot," and "anti-Semite."

The reality is that antiwhites are not being hypocritical, because the pretext that *"nonwhites and their opinions are important and deserve to be yielded or deferred to"* only applies when that pretext can be used to inflict harm on Westernkind and Western Civilization.

When a nonwhite conservative espouses conservative positions, he or she is inhibiting the infliction of harm on Westernkind and Western Civilization and is therefore condemned as "evil" by antiwhites—as well as all the words antiwhites deem synonyms of evil.

Tweets and emails abound comparing antiwhite responses to two different events, which to fair-minded people appear hypocritical. For example, how many tweets have you seen comparing two tweets from the same blue check-marked account with one tweet applauding identity politics for nonwhites and the other tweet condemning white identity?

"Hypocrite!" is the response over and over. However, once you ignore antiwhite pretexts—once you understand the true motivations of an antiwhite, you will see that antiwhites are never hypocritical. They are always acting to inflict harm on Westernkind and Western Civilization.

Identify—Immunize—Go Free

MPs That Are New to You:

You now have the means of defense against MPs. You know how to Confront, Challenge, and Dispel (CCD) MPs and how to use meme-curatives (MCs). You know to filter the Regime's messaging through the Antiwhite Screed to clearly identify the true antiwhite objectives. You understand that you have one victimizer—the antiwhite. These tools help you Go Free from the MPs you are already infected with, but they also give you the means to immunize yourself against new infections.

The Regime develops new MPs. They resurrect MPs they abandoned. They modify and amend MPs to reuse them. They also develop **meme-pathogen montages (MPMs)**— linking several MPs together. An example of a MPM is the combined use of the MPs *"hate speech," "micro-aggressions,"* and *"structural racism"* to hinder and prohibit white positive speech at institutions of higher learning.

Messages (images, ideas, or arguments) contain MPs within them when they are directly or indirectly harmful to our people. Basically, anything that white-guilts, imposes one-sided morally-, intellectually-, or emotionally-based harmful obligations on us, or otherwise weakens our people in any way is an MP.

Sometimes it is easy to identify new MPs because the "cause and effect" are simple and direct: *"The West's need for fossil fuel is destroying the planet." "Institutional racism undermines nonwhite academic and professional achievement and happiness."* These MPs clearly equate Westernkind with negative outcomes. These MPs induce white-guilt and "legitimize" the harm antiwhites inflict on us.

However, there are more sophisticated and less obvious MPs. They may encourage Westmen to think or act in ways that seem neutral, but are—in fact—harmful to Westernkind. Such MPs are intentionally crafted to slip into your mind as a piece of a larger message, such as a news report, TV show or movie, or academic discourse. If you fail to identify the MP in the larger message, you will be infected without realizing it.

These more sophisticated MPs may be *two, three, or even four* deductions removed from the original message. Let's look at an example. A few years ago, antiwhites spread the MP that *"Mexicans are suffering atrocities—of every description—at the hands of Mexican criminals armed with American firearms."*

Those criminals obtained firearms in the United States. They were able to do so because America has a right to self-defense, enforced by America's constitutional right to keep and bear arms. As whites created America and wrote its Constitution, and as most whites celebrate, exercise, and defend the right to keep and bear arms against antiwhite efforts to cripple the Second Amendment, the inescapable conclusion was that *"whites are to blame for nonwhites suffering in Mexico"*: Firearms are available in America because of Westmen. Mexican criminals obtain firearms in America. Mexican criminals victimize Mexicans in Mexico with those firearms.

Often, new MPs are built on or linked to existing MPs to magnify their potency and infectivity. In the example above, the MP *"Mexicans are suffering atrocities at the hands of Mexican criminals armed with American firearms"* was linked by implication to the older MP *"white gun culture is responsible for the suffering and deaths of American nonwhites"* who use firearms when committing crimes.

The MP *"Mexicans are suffering atrocities at the hands of Mexican criminals armed with American firearms"* was "validated" by—and in turn gave "validation" to—the MP *"white gun culture is responsible for the suffering and deaths of American nonwhites."* Each supported and "validated" the other, furthering the Antiwhite Narrative.

This process of linking to older MPs increases the potency of new MPs by triggering MPs that you are already infected with. *The triggered MP reduces your ability to resist new infections by undermining rational examination of the new MP.*

It undermines conscious and critical examination by occupying your mind with the older MPs' interpretive mandates—the thoughts and emotions associated with the older MPs.

Building Immunity:

Once you have identified a new MP, you immunize yourself against it in the same way you combat an MP you are infected with: CCD as soon as you are exposed.

For example, when first hearing the *"Mexican atrocities are caused by America's right to self-defense"* MP, tell yourself that this message is an MP and therefore antiwhite. Tell yourself that Mexican criminals are to blame for their behavior. Most importantly, remind yourself that antiwhites want to white-guilt you and turn you against White Wellbeing.

Remind yourself—in every case—that the antiwhite ideas, concepts, feelings, etc. that well up within you are the "smoking gun" evidence of the crimes antiwhites have committed against you, everyone you love, and our people. Use the righteous anger you generate from these moments to vigorously combat that part of yourself that remains infected, that continues to do the bidding of your victimizers long after they infected you.

When confronted with a new MP that is linked to one or more MPs that you are already infected with, *you must CCD both the new and old MPs*, immunizing yourself against the new while treating yourself for the old.

For example, substantial financial grants and tax assistance are offered by NGOs (largely funded with our tax dollars) and the federal and state governments to nonwhite immigrants to enable them to buy and/or start businesses in the US, such as "individual development grants." If this information became widely known, antiwhites would spread new MPs, such as *"immigrant 'restitution' packages create American jobs."*

This new MP would trigger old MPs, such as *"nonwhite immigration improves the American economy"* and *"the white race has to make up (pay restitution) for the harm that Western Civilization has inflicted on the nonwhite world."* All of these MPs must be CCDed as the new one is encountered and the old ones are triggered.

Finally, by memorizing the MCs that I provide, you will develop a baseline of immunity that will serve you as a powerful foundation from which to combat MPs that are new to you. This process of memorizing MCs is especially powerful for our youngest children, as the deeper the foundations are laid for Wellbeing, the harder it is for MP infections to take root in their subconscious minds.

Refer to and memorize the MCs in Appendices A and B. Doing so is far—FAR—more important to your health than good hygiene, healthy diet, exercise, vitamin C, legitimate vaccinations, refraining from illicit drug abuse, etc.

Your Examples of CCDing New MPs

In your own words, give three examples of CCDs you could make in response to the MP that *"Western educational expectations undermine nonwhite self-confidence, and thereby sabotage nonwhite achievement."* Focus at least one of your answers on the fact that antiwhites want to infect and white-guilt us with MPs to suppress White Wellbeing:

Confrontation—Strategy—Action:

Never Defend Against

Antiwhite Attacks

It may surprise you, but one of the most important lessons you have to learn is to *never defend yourself against antiwhite verbal attacks.*

We live in a world dominated by antiwhites and antiwhite social dictates. This creates a significant advantage for antiwhites in every debate. The Antiwhite Narrative and environment in which we live forces debate to begin from antiwhite baselines. Antiwhite professionals from a host of disciplines related to persuasion have and continue to arm antiwhites with an arsenal of weaponized words and deceptive argumentation tactics designed to force their victims onto the defensive. These include antiwhite slurs (racist, supremacist, fascist), equivalence fallacies, per capita fallacies, appeals to emotion, *non sequiturs*, exceptional cases, *ad hominem* attacks, etc.

However, the greatest adversary you face when verbally attacked by an antiwhite is yourself—your *own* MP infections. When you try to answer a deceptive antiwhite argument, your subconscious mind drowns your conscious mind with the same deceptive MPs that the antiwhite is using to attack you. Each of these MPs cripples your conscious mind with their associated interpretive mandates: emotions that condemn you as immoral for opposing antiwhite positions—emotions that also define your antiwhite attacker as moral.

Now, recall that your conscious mind is the slow biplane, while your subconscious is the supersonic jet. As a result, the MPs you are infected with ambush every conscious response you try to formulate. If you are honest with yourself, you will admit that you have struggled to formulate responses to antiwhite verbal attacks. You will recall witnessing the pained expressions on the faces of others who have tried to formulate responses to their antiwhite attackers.

When you are verbally attacked, your conscious mind clumsily fumbles from one ambushed thought to the next while your antiwhite attacker smugly gloats over you. When, for example, an antiwhite implies or calls you an antiwhite slur, such as "bigot," because you object to an antiwhite program that will discriminate against whites in favor of nonwhites, your conscious mind is instantly filled with the thoughts and emotions associated with the MPs related to the topic. For example, those who want to favor nonwhites at the expense of whites are *"honorable, intelligent, selfless, and attractive—they are doing the right thing."* Those who disagree are *"dishonorable, unintelligent, selfish, and ugly."*

Unwillingly, and often unwittingly, your mind instantly places the antiwhite in the moral, positive category and you in the immoral, negative category. You are also instantly aware that anyone observing the disagreement has also placed the antiwhite and you in the same positive and negative categories.

Trying to formulate responses while your mind is flooded with these antiwhite thoughts, emotions, and observations is nearly impossible. To compound your disadvantage, the antiwhite is able to "prove" his point by merely citing MPs, and until Going Free, you were disarmed in such debates. For example, the antiwhite might say, *"We are a nation of immigrants."* Before Going Free, your response was likely cumbersome and ineffective. Now, you know to say, *"That's antiwhite. Whites can't be immigrants to Western Civilization because the West only exists in us. It only exists because we exist."*

It is common for Westmen to grope for justifications to such easily defensible positions as whether or not Westernkind exists, or even if it deserves to exist. Such fumbling represents the deep psychological scars of our physical, mental, and spiritual abuse.

Going on the defensive makes you look and feel weak because in the defensive you are weak. The best defense against an antiwhite attack is a counter-attack. Go on the offensive with MCs. Follow the examples below of incorrect and correct responses.

Antiwhite Attack: *"We have to let minorities into the country. Don't you have any compassion?"*

Defensive responses (incorrect):

- *"I am a compassionate person, but..."*
- *"We are compassionate in all these ways..."*
- *"We can do more to help them in their own countries..."*
- *"We can't continue to be compassionate to nonwhites if..."*

Whether or not any of these arguments are true does not matter. All that matters is that these arguments are defensive in nature.

Offensive MCs (correct):

- *"That's antiwhite..."*
- *"Why do you hate Western Civilization so much that you want white erasure?"*
- *"Why do you want to change white communities into places that are uncomfortable and dangerous for us?"*
- *"Why do you want to endanger white children?"*
- *"Why do you want to make it harder for whites to pay for their groceries, health insurance,"* etc.

Always answer an antiwhite *accusation* with an *accusation*!

Antiwhite: *"You hate minorities."*

Wellbeing Advocate: *"You hate Westmen."*

Antiwhite: *"You think minorities are predisposed to criminality."*

Wellbeing Advocate: *"You think whites are predisposed to criminality."*

Antiwhite: *"You think minority culture is inferior."*

Wellbeing Advocate: *"You think Western Culture is inferior."*

Antiwhite: *"You want whites to be superior."*

Wellbeing Advocate: *"You want nonwhites to be superior."*

Never defend! Always attack!

Face Antiwhitism

Facing antiwhitism is an exercise for developing and deepening the knowledge and skillsets you have acquired by Going Free. Facing antiwhitism increases your confidence and breaks your fear of expressing skepticism and disagreement. Moreover, by facing antiwhitism, you learn to withdraw the "moral authority" you have given the Regime.

You have learned to think of the Regime as *"my country," "my government," "my church," "my alma mater,"* and so forth. You have given it your obedience, faith, love, and loyalty, but the Regime is harmful to our people and therefore you as an individual. You owe it nothing. Obey its laws because the antiwhites will punish and imprison us for the slightest infraction, but when—in your heart—you rescind your obedience, faith, love, and loyalty, when you reorient yourself to White Wellbeing, you and our people benefit in innumerable ways.

The internet is an excellent place to face antiwhitism. Your first step is to assume a nickname. Even if your opposition to antiwhitism is already public, a nickname will enable you to more fully express your thoughts and challenge antiwhitism than is possible using your real identity. A nickname will also enable you to build emotional strength and composure.

Once you have chosen a nickname, commit to challenging all manifestations of antiwhite thought, acts, and opinions on the internet. Identify, frequent, and post on video channels, articles, blogs and forums that address socio-political subjects related to antiwhitism, both directly and indirectly.

Examples:

- YouTube content producers who address socio-political subjects.
- Bloggers who write movie reviews.
- Forums dedicated to parenting.
- News websites where authors twist their coverage to conform to the Antiwhite Narrative.

Identify and face antiwhitism across a spectrum of opinion. "Right wing" writers/presenters are usually not as antiwhite as those on the "left," but all antiwhitism threatens White Wellbeing and must be challenged.

Resolve to identify, frequent, and post several times a week. Again, facing antiwhitism is like building muscle—you must continually workout to reap the rewards.

However, do not limit your efforts to the internet. Think about how you can counter the Antiwhite Narrative in your local or personal sphere. You can purchase ad space in your local paper. You can post flyers at your local grocery store. Write a letter to your town's paper about a local antiwhite issue. Your letters to the editors are less likely to be published than those from antiwhites, but you will still benefit by exercising your new-found skills. There are nearly limitless ways you can criticize MPs and share your story of Going Free.

You can also face antiwhitism by creating white positive art. Use your newfound knowledge of Going Free, my livestreams and videos, and local/global events to write white positive prose and poetry; record white positive rock or synth, etc.; paint white positive paintings, carve white positive sculptures, and make white positive videography, etc. Look to my White Wellbeing Community playlists on my social media platforms to be inspired by the white positive art created by others.

Once you have anonymously developed some of your Going Free skills, begin facing antiwhitism in non-anonymous scenarios. Speak with those in your circles of influence who are likely or more likely to hold opinions that are similar to White Wellbeing. Carefully select people who are less likely or less able to harm you for sharing thoughts that are not antiwhite.

Remember, discussing any deviation from antiwhitism can be contentious. Do not allow frustration to cause you to lose your temper, as such discussions can become verbally combative under those circumstances.

You must focus on projecting positivity—white positivity. Do not allow your inexperience to drive you into frustrated impatience and **white negative** language, because you will then look like the villain in the Antiwhite Narrative.

Recall that we are concerned with love, hope and redemption. Our brothers and sisters are sick with MPs. They need our help, and we begin helping them by slowly introducing some new words to their vocabulary: antiwhite; antiwhitism; Westernkind; hush crime; Antiwhite Narrative; White Wellbeing, etc.

Share a piece of news that affords you an opportunity to introduce one of these words. For example, *"Did you hear about that new law that discriminates against our people? I can't believe how antiwhite the system has become."* Or, *"Yeah, critical race theory is bad, but it is only one piece of antiwhitism."*

Start small; inject a word here or there. Develop your skills. Reflect after every discussion whether you feel like you did well or not. Review *Go Free*: Did you take the right approach? Did you use the right MC? Did you stay in *our* story?

Consistently apply your new skills to your life and review, review, review. In time, you will notice latent strengths rising to the surface. You will become a better you—a better loved one—a better worker—a better advocate for yourself, your family, and our people.

Your Examples of Retorts

Give three possible retorts you would use when confronted with the antiwhite slander that Westmen "stole" America from nonwhites. Remember, go on the offensive: What is the antiwhite trying to do to you, your well-being and the well-being of our people by making this allegation?

Keep it Promethean (KIP)

The **Promethean** rule to **KIP** means that Wellbeing advocates live their lives and frame their thoughts to comport with the dignity and honorable behavior of the Prometheans in **Prometheus Rising**, that reason, logic, and evidence are at the core of decision making and interpretation, and that Going Free is central to their lives.

As ambassadors and champions of our rapidly growing community (or in the phraseology of Prometheus Rising, the Prometheum, which is the Promethean community), advocates for White Wellbeing KIP when they acknowledge that Westernkind is a victimized people—persecuted, exploited, and physically, mentally, and spiritually abused. A Wellbeing advocate regards bringing harm to his fellow advocates as unforgivably shameful because such an act victimizes the victim.

As many doctrines and activities are detrimental to the AAP, White Wellbeing advocates not only identify antiwhite judgments and mores as harmful, but they also KIP when they guard against seemingly compatible or sympathetic doctrines and activities that might indirectly undermine or interfere with the process of Going Free.

For example, some content producers in white sympathetic spheres behave no better than tabloid journalists. They give explanations and take positions on historical and contemporary events for the self-serving purposes of getting attention and donations—not because these explanations and positions will benefit you or our people.

When you repeat what content producers say, you are making a **reputational investment**. If you repeat the self-serving content of such content producers to your friends and family, you burn your reputation to ashes. Typically, within a few weeks or months such content producers recant with a new set of exotic attention-getting explanations and positions, but your reputation is permanently destroyed.

As the success of Going Free is success and freedom for Westernkind, to KIP is to ensure the rapid growth and success of our community.

Continuing Your Journey:

Fellowship with Others Going Free

Fellowshipping with others Going Free will benefit you in a great many ways. The feeling of kinship with others Going Free will warm your heart in ways that you have never felt before. Discussing Going Free with such people will improve and deepen your understanding of the process.

Get yourself what Mr. V., from the White Wellbeing community, calls a Going Free friend (GFF). Such people will have insights you will have missed, and you will have insights they will have overlooked. Your fellowship will build knowledge and understanding that would otherwise have been beyond reach.

You may also form a **Go Free club (GFC)**. These clubs may meet virtually, in person, or both. While GFCs are not centrally organized, run, or operated by Jason Köhne, they will be recognized if they operate according to Going Free protocol: The sole purpose and function of GFCs is to facilitate and expedite the process of Going Free, practicing the exercises, lexicon, and dialectics of Going Free as well as organizing the spread of Going Free online and by way of flyer drops.

Share Your Story of Going Free

and Accelerate Your Gains!

Frequently sharing your experiences of Going Free will help you accelerate your gains. It will also help those you share your experiences with. Tell others about the improvements you are seeing in your life as a result of Going Free. Compare and contrast the benefits of Going Free with other white sympathetic and self-improvement approaches. Tell people about your life prior to Going Free and contrast that with how far you have come. Tell them about all the people in your life that you couldn't reach with other white sympathetic messages, and then tell them about how you used Going Free to bring these people to white positivity. As you improve your ability to voice your gains, your understanding and grasp of the process will grow—your journey will help others to begin theirs.

Go Free Every Day:

Regularly Review the AAP

Dependent on the prevalence of antiwhitism in your life, the length of time you were exposed, and the severity of your infection, it is easy to backslide. It is easy to fall into the pitfalls of self-defeating perspectives and superstitions.

To Go Free, you must regularly review the AAP to ensure that you are engaging antiwhites and antiwhite arguments with the proper perspectives and MCs. You want to develop good technique and this requires regular practice. It requires examining your interactions and deepening your subconscious alignment to the AAP.

We will continue to be imprisoned in antiwhite environments for the foreseeable future. The Regime will continue to attack and infect us with MPs every single day. In response, you must make a daily commitment to Go Free every—single—day.

You are either Going Free, or you are backsliding. You are growing in physical, mental, and spiritual health, or regressing—degenerating toward physical, mental, and spiritual decay. There is no equilibrium. There is no standing idle. You must constantly refresh and expand your knowledge of Going Free until it becomes subconscious and implicit—an indelible part of your identity.

Personal Changes Since Completing L3 of Going Free

If you have applied yourself diligently to the process of Going Free, you will have noticed positive changes in your life. Some of you will be in a state of elementary awareness and growth. Others will feel themselves hurtling toward enlightenment and alignment with the archetype. All experiences are valid and part of the healing process.

Where are you in that process? How much clearer is your understanding of the world?

How does it feel to be equipped with tools to heal and defend yourself?

Are you like most at this stage in the journey of Going Free, able to see the intent to inflict harm on Westernkind behind antiwhite pretexts?

Do you enjoy the feeling of empowerment by knowing the secret motivations behind antiwhite thought and behavior? How much more confident do you feel in your ability to debate them?

How much of your confusion has been cleared away by learning the true nature of our victimization?

Has acquiring the means to continue your self-improvement excited you?

How clearly do you sense the improvements in your health, emotional state, clarity of mind, and spiritual empowerment?

Give three examples of how you have benefited by Going Free thus far:

Take the Next Step

You have come a long way. You have learned the hidden motivations behind the antiwhite hatred for Westernkind. You have learned new concepts that will facilitate your journey to Go Free. You know how to identify MPs in the environment and in yourself, and how they can harm you and lead to white-noir. You have begun training your perception, and this ability will sharpen overtime.

You know how to address MPs as you encounter or sense them within yourself—treating and weakening them as you grow stronger. You know how to immunize yourself against new MPs. You have developed behaviors that will erode the foundations by which you are easily infected and swayed.

You have begun aligning with the archetype of Westernkind. But the real excitement is yet to come. Further breakthroughs await you at higher levels of Going Free— new opportunities for growth and power. The skillsets you acquired by completing L1 through L3 enable you to receive further instruction. You are now able to climb higher toward your physical, mental, and spiritual potential.

The next step in your journey is *Born Guilty: Liable for Compensation, Subject to Retaliation.* This text invites you into my study in The Plains, Virginia. Over a two-day period, I speak to you in the first person, sharing instructive events from my life.

You will find both fiction and nonfiction stories in the books of *Prometheus Rising* and *Crucible* respectively, which are contained within *Born Guilty.* You will dream and glimpse images that further vivify you, aligning you with the archetype. You will unleash your abilities as a Westman— abilities unrivaled in world history.

Read *Born Guilty* with the knowledge you have acquired, and you will have prepared yourself for the next step in your journey to Go Free. Healing, purpose, progress, safety, and happiness await you.

Lastly, a practitioner of Going Free, would like to leave you with a final thought as you reflect on this passage from *Born Guilty*:

"We have a special role in the world. There is no Western Civilization without Westernkind, and no other civilization has done more to benefit and elevate humanity.
The world needs us to be proud, to do what we do best: to create order from chaos, knowledge from ignorance, liberty from tyranny, comfort from suffering, beauty from ugliness. The world needs us."

Going Free practitioner: *"The world needs you."*

Appendices

Glossary

Note: This glossary contains additional terms that are used on Jason Köhne's *Go Free* livestreams. Show dates and times are available at NoWhiteGuilt.org.

- **abstractionist:** A <u>saboteur</u> who advocates for ideas rather than the people who create and sustain the ideas, as exemplified by those who advocate **Western** culture (Western philosophy, law and order, economy, civility, morals, etc.) without advocating for **Westernkind**.

- **antagonist:** A <u>saboteur</u> who *plays the villain*, assuming the forms, language, and appearance of the "bad guy" in the **Antiwhite Narrative**.

- **antiwhite:** Relating to or characterized by **antiwhitism**. A descriptor for thoughts, actions, laws/policies/rules, individuals and organizations hostile to **Westernkind**. Also a term for antiwhite individuals: "an antiwhite," "antiwhites."

- **antiwhite lens:** A perspective promoted by **antiwhites** that leads to antiwhite conclusions. E.g. selectively ignoring or minimizing the suffering of **Westmen** while emphasizing the suffering of nonwhites, or holding Westmen to higher standards of morality and agency while providing endless excuses for the behaviors of nonwhites.

- **Antiwhite Narrative:** The dominant narrative in the West, wherein **Westmen** are the antagonists and **antiwhites** are the protagonists. A product of **antiwhitism**, the **Antiwhite Narrative** is imposed on Western Civilization by antiwhites who dominate the nerve centers of the **Regime**.

- **antiwhite oligarch(s):** An extraordinarily wealthy and/or powerful **antiwhite**. Do not refer to such people as "elites" because by doing so you subordinate yourself to them in various categories: intelligence, refinement, etc.

- **antiwhite precept:** The first of the two components of an **MP**. The **antiwhite** precept of an MP is the actual antiwhite belief, that is on some level of consciousness accepted as true by the mind. E.g. *"***Westmen*** didn't create Western Civilization, they stole it."* The second component of the MP, the **interpretive mandate**, dictates an emotional response to the precept.

- **Antiwhite Screed:** An **MC** tool/formula to understand and predict **antiwhite** thoughts and behavior. (*Ceteris paribus*, or excluding unusual circumstances:) *"Everything conducive to White Wellbeing is negative. Conversely, everything antithetic to White Wellbeing is positive."*

- **antiwhite slur:** Derogatory labels that directly or indirectly inflict harm on **White Wellbeing** or those serving it. For example, the word "racist" is an antiwhite slur. Antiwhite slurs are individual pieces of the *language* *of white oppression/***white erasure**, which is reinforced and legitimized by its use.

- **antiwhite tribunal:** Any **antiwhite** or group of antiwhites that sit in judgment, meting punishment for **heresy** to antiwhitism.

- **antiwhitism:** Thoughts, actions and policies hostile to **Westernkind**.

- **Archetype Alignment Protocol (AAP):** A practice that aligns **Westmen** with the archetype of **Westernkind**, which—among other objectives—unleashes the indomitable Western Spirit within them. This process is called **Going Free**. Aligning with the archetype is the goal of Going Free.

- **bio-spirit:** Crudely defined as instinct, bio-spirit is the natural, historic, and expected thought and behavioral patterns distinct to a people.

- **bio-spiritual expression:** The broadly recognizable expressions of each race of man, which projected onto their environments are their **cultures**. Bio-spiritual expression—as it intersects with environment—is synonymous with the word "culture".

- **bio-spiritual incompatibility:** The irreconcilability of **bio-spiritual expressions** among the peoples of man. Bio-spiritual incompatibility precludes multiracial societies, as bio-spiritual discomfort is the basis of violent balkanization.

- **chimeras:** People and depictions of people (in art, children's toys, etc.) that are race and sexless.

- **Confront, Challenge, and Dispel (CCD):** An **AAP** technique by which **Wellbeing** advocates—cued and triggered by internal and external **MPs**—consciously create **counter triggers** in the subconscious mind by vocally or internally **counter asserting** with **MCs**.

- **counter asserting:** A step in the **CCD** technique wherein **MCs** are recited or created as countervailing statements (uttered vocally or internally) that aggressively counter an **MP**.

- **counter trigger:** A consciously created subconscious mechanism for the negation of **MPs** and **white-noir**. Counter triggers are triggered by the triggered MPs with which a person is infected.

- **craven:** A **saboteur** who encourages **white flight** or draws **Wellbeing** advocates away from white positive communities by various means.

- **culture:** The **bio-spiritual expression** of a race of people projected onto their environment and reflected back from that environment.

- **curative contagion:** An ancillary term for the **AAP** (**Going Free**), referencing an aspect of the AAPs design that enables it to spread easily from person to person.

- **doom dissector:** A content producer who endlessly discusses and analyzes the harm that **antiwhites** are inflicting on **Westmen** and Western Civilization.

- **doom documenter:** A content producer who reports on all the harm that **antiwhites** are inflicting on **Westmen** and Western Civilization.

- **face antiwhitism:** An **AAP** technique by which **Wellbeing** advocates exercise, develop, deepen, and explore the knowledge and skillsets they have acquired for **Going Free**. The technique involves challenging **antiwhitism** and sharing personal success stories in Internet forums, community newspapers, etc.

- **fantasist:** A **doom documenter** and/or **doom dissector** who frightens his or her audience for the purpose of ensnaring that audience with a false solution.

- **forced multiracial harmonizing:** Efforts designed to ameliorate the progressive tension/hostility between racial/ethnic groups in racially/ethnically diverse populations. Such efforts take various forms and consume massive resources in time, money, energy, and intelligence.

- **Going Free:** The application and practice of **AAP**. Aligning with the archetype of **Westernkind** is the goal of Going Free.

- **Going Free club (GFC):** An independent club whose participants gather for the purpose of **Going Free** as well as helping others to Go Free.

- **Going Free friend (GFF):** A fellow **Going Free** practitioner with whom a Going Free practitioner *exercises*, discussing the lexicon and dialectics of Go Free and practicing the exercises for mutual benefit.

- **Great White Awakening:** The Great White Awakening, Great White Rising, Union Europa and White Renaissance is the synergistic and exponential momentum manifested by **Westmen Going Free** in escalating numbers, marked by milestones that signify the increasing impossibility of arresting momentum.

- **hate hoax:** Any covert act—committed by one or more **antiwhites** in the guise of a white person or people—that conforms to the **Antiwhite Narrative** and thereby demonizes **Westmen** is a hate hoax. Hate hoaxes draw the noose of suspicion around the throats of all white people, and thereby are "hate crimes" against our entire race. Such crimes are used to "justify" past, present, and future harm to **Westernkind**.

- **heresy:** Deviation from **antiwhitism**.

- **hush crime:** All acts that victimize one or more **Westmen**, and by so doing contradict and/or disprove the **Antiwhite Narrative**, and are therefore obfuscated, lied about, downplayed, ignored, or given comparatively little publicity/attention by **antiwhites**. Not all hush crimes are "criminal"; some are legal but socially condemned acts. Debunked **hate hoaxes** routinely become hush crimes. Hush crime is a powerful **MC** because the premise reveals the truth about antiwhite domination of **Regime** news and entertainment media.

- **interpretive mandate:** The second of the two components of an **MP**. The interpretive mandate of an MP is a form of mental programming that dictates how we are supposed to feel about the first component of an MP: the **antiwhite precept**. E.g. the interpretive mandate could mandate that the infected person feel negative emptions such as guilt in association with a precept that slanders **Westernkind** as wicked, or to feel more positive emotions such as righteousness or good humor in association with a precept that advocates inflicting harm on Westernkind.

- **isolationist:** A **craven saboteur** promoting the "bunker mindset": the destructive belief that the best course for **White Wellbeing** is isolating one's family with several other families on small farmsteads in "remote" territories.

- **jealousy and envy:** The fundamental motivations of the **antiwhite**. Envy is specifically delineated from jealousy as a feeling of discontent/resentment/covetousness of **Westernkind's** successes, possessions, history, etc., whereas jealousy is anger/rage for a perceived rival who has or is likely to triumph in competition.

- **Keep it Promethean (KIP):** An **AAP** technique by which **Wellbeing** advocates live their lives and frame their thoughts so as not to conflict with **Going Free**. It means that Wellbeing advocates serve the welfare of the community for **White Wellbeing** (In the phraseology of **Prometheus Rising**, **Prometheans** serve the well-being of the Prometheum, which is the Promethean community.), ensuring the rapid growth, dissemination, and success of our community. White Wellbeing advocates acknowledge that **Westernkind** is the most victimized people—persecuted, exploited, and psychologically abused for the totality of their lives. As such, to KIP means that Wellbeing advocates consider transgressions against **Westmen** (who are not **antiwhite**) to be shameful and disgraceful beyond compare.

- **meme-curative (MC):** A thought or idea that helps to remedy **MPs**. Includes useful concepts, such as "**numerical courage**," "**forced multiracial harmonizing**," and statements, such as *"there is no excellence where there is equality."*

- **meme-pathogen (MP):** A thought or idea that is destructive for the individual or group who holds it. In the practice of **Going Free**, MPs mostly refer specifically to **antiwhite** MPs: thoughts or ideas that produce physical, mental, emotional, or spiritual disease in **Westernkind**. They are *lesions* on our bodies, minds, and spirits. For example, any belief that **white-guilts** or imposes one-sided moral, intellectual, or sentimental obligations on us that weaken our people in any way is an MP.

- **meme-pathogen montage (MPM):** **MPs** used in combination to support (and seemingly validate) each other.

- **mercenary:** A type of **saboteur** with three distinct variants: **professional agents**, **opportunists**, and **repentant villains**.

- **moralize, intellectualize, sentimentalize (MIS):** The pretexts (and the creation of such pretexts) employed by **antiwhites** to "legitimize" and "justify" the harm they inflict on **Westmen** and Western Civilization. To *MIS pretext* is to create, cite, repeat, etc. antiwhite pretexts.

- **multiracial harmonizing:** See the preferred wording: **forced multiracial harmonizing**.

- **numerical courage:** The state in which a people, within the body of another people or peoples, confidently projects their **bio-spirit** onto their environment without concern for the other people or peoples. The point at which nonwhites within **Western** countries manifest and project their **bio-spiritual expressions** (which are at variance with white expression) onto Western Civilization. This process initiates a cultural arms race which always ends in oppressive governmental tyranny and violent balkanization.

- **numerical diffidence:** The state in which a people, within the body of another people or peoples, is reluctant to project their **bio-spirit** onto their environment for fear of upsetting/angering the other people or peoples. Prior to achieving **numerical courage**, nonwhites in **Western** countries are in a state of numerical diffidence. While in this state, nonwhites superficially conform to the **bio-spiritual expression** of **Westernkind**.

- **opportunist:** A variant of the **mercenary saboteur**. Someone who joins or befriends **white sympathetic communities** with the intent of severing ties and "telling their story" for attention and financial reward from an **antiwhite** world eager to bolster the **Antiwhite Narrative**.

- **pervasive antiwhitism:** The social, moral/ethical, and legal imperatives with which **antiwhites** have structured society so as to advance, enrich, and empower nonwhites at the expense of, detriment to, and ruination of whites.

- **potential-to-power (PTP):** The aggregate of one's **bio-spiritual** potentialities to manifest, attain, and satisfy one's desires. PTP is limited by internal and external factors: Internally, one's unique bio-spiritual composition or architecture establishes one's potentialities. External forces—specifically **MPs**—undermine the attainment of internal potentialities by inflicting **white-noir**—reducing one's abilities to manifest, attain, and satisfy one's desires. PTP can be positively and negatively influenced throughout life. By **Going Free** and reducing white-noir, one increases one's PTP.

- **pristine:** Places/people/states of mind/things inside **Western** societies that are largely untainted by **antiwhitism** and unaffected by white erasure, having *remained in* or possibly *returned to* the "pristine" state they historically were in.

- **professional agent:** A variant of the **mercenary saboteur**. A member of organized **antiwhite** operations designed to infiltrate and harm **white sympathetic communities**.

- **Promethean:** A person who is **Going Free**. Also an adjective meaning to be befitting of someone Going Free. In reference to the dignity and honorable behavior of the Prometheans in **Prometheus Rising**.

- **Prometheus Rising:** A book by Jason Köhne presenting an inspirational and edifying myth, crafted for the advancement of **Westernkind**.

- **quicksanding:** The behavior of dismissing ideas that either do or might **serve White Wellbeing** without due consideration. From the allegory that a person behaving in this way is like quicksand, "sinking" all ideas put to them.

- **Regime:** The governments, national and international banks, news and entertainment media, academia and all institutions influenced by these entities.

- **repentant villain:** A role inside the **Antiwhite Narrative**, played by former **antagonists**. The repentant villain expresses or feels remorse for playing the villain, and (never having truly rejected the Antiwhite Narrative) "repents" by assuming this complementary destructive role. The repentant villain may silently renounce and abandon **white sympathetic** concerns, or become actively **antiwhite** (possibly becoming a **mercenary** in the process).

- **reputational investment:** Putting one's reputation on the line by repeating the thoughts of content producers to one's friends and family.

- **road blocking:** Any speech or activity, such as **support shaming** and **virtue trapping**, which undermines—in any way—a **Wellbeing** advocate's work for **White Wellbeing**.

- **saboteur:** A person who intentionally or unintentionally inflicts negative influence on **white sympathetic communities** from within. Types of saboteur described include **mercenaries, cravens, isolationists, abstractionists, sectarianists**, and **antagonists**.

- **sectarianist:** A **saboteur** who divides and weakens the community.

- **serve White Wellbeing or serve Wellbeing:** To improve the lives and structural supports of **Westernkind** and its expressions.

- **shame extorting:** Instilling shame to extort money for legal and other expenses from **white sympathetic** people after engaging in high risk/low reward behavior that harmed or could have harmed **White Wellbeing**—even when the behavior is claimed to have been in service to the white race.

- **social lynching:** Economic, social, and psychological attacks zealously inflicted by **antiwhites** on those who intentionally or unintentionally express opinions, or engage in acts at variance with **antiwhitism**. Social lynching often results in alienation from family and friends, as well as loss of employment and therefore all of the concomitant losses, i.e., standard of living, health care, insurance, home, automobile, etc.

- **spousing:** Entering the **white positive sphere** with the intent of finding a quality mate with which to abandon the white positive sphere.

- **support shaming:** Criticizing an advocate for **White Wellbeing**—with the intent to undermine his or her efforts for White Wellbeing—for accepting and/or asking for various forms of support: volunteer, financial, etc. Note: withholding or questioning support to newcomers to the **white positive sphere** is not support shaming. Such individuals have to prove themselves worthy of support with self-sacrifice and a history of successful advocacy for White Wellbeing.

- **tactical frames of thought (TFTs):** Another term for **meme-curatives (MCs)**.

- **thought chain(s):** A construct that engenders derivative constructs: thoughts/premises that naturally lead to other thoughts/conclusions. For example, **MCs** triggering related MCs; or **MPs** triggering related MPs.

- **vague(s):** People who have not come into contact with any form of **antiwhitism**, or those who are not firmly **antiwhite** but who speak, write and act (**villainy signal**) in ways that conform to the **Antiwhite Narrative**.

- **villainy signaling:** Signaling compliance with antiwhitism. A behavior sometimes inappropriately described as *virtue* signaling.

- **virtue trapping:** Criticizing an advocate for **White Wellbeing**—with the intent to undermine his or her efforts for White Wellbeing—for not "perfectly" exemplifying a virtue that **Wellbeing** advocates maintain as necessary for a healthy life and community.

- **Wellbeing:** Another term for **White Wellbeing**. Sometimes used as a pithier descriptor for something that **serves White Wellbeing**, such as Wellbeing art (art that serves White Wellbeing), and Wellbeing advocates (people who **serve White Wellbeing**).

- **Western:** Of **Westernkind**.

- **Westernkind:** White people as a collective and as a historical entity.

- **Westman:** A white person.

- **Westmen:** White people and white people as a collective.

- **white-erase:** To inflict **white erasure**.

- **white-erased history:** Rewritten history to conform to the **Antiwhite Narrative** and facilitate **white erasure**.

- **white erasure:** When to the detriment of **White Wellbeing**: The removal, rewriting, renaming, defacing, expunging, etc. of anything related to or of **Westernkind**.

- **white flight:** White individuals or groups fleeing—physically or mentally—from discomfort, such as **bio-spiritual** disharmony, physical danger by **antiwhites**, **white-guilt**, **white-noir**, etc. White flight is a stress response or coping mechanism. Examples are moving one's place of residence; quietism; drug use; self-mutilation; dating and marrying nonwhites, and committing biological white erasure. The ultimate form of white flight is suicide.

- **white-guilt:** One of the most destructive elements of **white-noir**, white-guilt infects **Westmen** with culpability for the real and fabricated "wrongdoings" of Westmen throughout history. It obligates us to pay a "debt" and "make amends" by way of surrender, atonement, and suffering. White-guilt develops in Westmen as a result of being white-guilted by **antiwhites**. Also used as a verb, meaning "to inflict white-guilt": white-guilting.

- **white ill-being:** A colloquial term used occasionally to mean the opposite of **White Wellbeing**.

- **white negative:** Having concern for the well-being of **Westernkind**, manifested negatively and destructively, often to the detriment of Westernkind, such as by adopting the role of villain in the **Antiwhite Narrative**. **White positive** and white negative are opposite poles of **white sympathetic**.

- **white-noir:** Multidimensional and pervasive physical, mental, emotional, and spiritual trauma suffered by **Westmen** as a consequence of **MP** infection and living in **antiwhite** societies.

- **white positive:** Having concern for the well-being of **Westernkind**, manifested positively and constructively, without adopting the role of villain in the **Antiwhite Narrative**.

- **white positive community:** A community of **white positive** individuals. In the context of **Going Free**, *our* white positive community refers to the Going Free community.

- **white positive sphere:** The totality of **white positive** individuals, ideas, communities, and entities.

- **white sympathetic:** Having concern for the welfare of **Westernkind**. (White sympathetic individuals who adopt a positive and constructive expression of their concern for

Westernkind by avoiding playing into the **Antiwhite Narrative** are also **white positive**.)

- **white sympathetic community:** A community of **white sympathetic** individuals.

- **white sympathetic sphere:** The totality of **white sympathetic** individuals, ideas, communities, and entities, including all implicit and explicit white sympathetics as well as **white negative** and **white positive** speech and behavior.

- **White Wellbeing:** The welfare of **Westernkind** and its expressions.

List of Abbreviations

- **(AAP) Archetype Alignment Protocol:** A practice that aligns **Westmen** with the archetype of **Westernkind**, which—among other objectives—unleashes the indomitable Western Spirit within them. This process is called **Going Free**. Aligning with the archetype is the goal of Going Free.

- **(CCD) Confront, Challenge, and Dispel:** An **AAP** technique by which **Wellbeing** advocates—cued and triggered by internal and external **MPs**—consciously create **counter triggers** in the subconscious mind by vocally or internally **counter asserting** with **MCs**.

- **(GFC) Going Free club:** An independent club whose participants gather for the purpose of **Going Free** as well as helping others to Go Free.

- **(GFF) Going Free friend:** A fellow **Going Free** practitioner with whom a Going Free practitioner *exercises*, discussing the lexicon and dialectics of Go Free and practicing the exercises for mutual benefit.

- **(KIP) Keep it Promethean:** An **AAP** technique by which **Wellbeing** advocates live their lives and frame their thoughts so as not to conflict with **Going Free**. It means that Wellbeing advocates serve the welfare of the community for **White Wellbeing** (In the phraseology of

Prometheus Rising, Prometheans serve the well-being of the Prometheum, which is the Promethean community.), ensuring the rapid growth, dissemination, and success of our community. White Wellbeing advocates acknowledge that **Westernkind** is the most victimized people— persecuted, exploited, and psychologically abused for the totality of their lives. As such, to KIP means that Wellbeing advocates consider transgressions against **Westmen** (who are not **antiwhite**) to be shameful and disgraceful beyond compare.

- **(MC) meme-curative:** A thought or idea that helps to remedy **MPs**. Includes useful concepts, such as "**numerical courage**," "**forced multiracial harmonizing**," and statements, such as *"there is no excellence where there is equality."*

- **(MIS) moralize, intellectualize, sentimentalize:** The pretexts (and the creation of such pretexts) employed by **antiwhites** to "legitimize" and "justify" the harm they inflict on **Westmen** and Western Civilization. To *MIS pretext* is to create, cite, repeat, etc. antiwhite pretexts.

- **(MP) meme-pathogen:** A thought or idea that is destructive for the individual or group who holds it. In the practice of **Going Free**, MPs mostly refer specifically to **antiwhite** MPs: thoughts or ideas that produce physical, mental, emotional, or spiritual disease in **Westernkind**. They are *lesions* on our bodies, minds, and spirits. For example, any belief that **<u>white-guilts</u>** or imposes one-sided moral, intellectual, or sentimental obligations on us that weaken our people in any way is an MP.

- **(MPM) meme-pathogen montage:** **<u>MPs</u>** used in combination to support (and seemingly validate) each other.

- **(PTP) potential-to-power:** The aggregate of one's **<u>bio-spiritual</u>** potentialities to manifest, attain, and satisfy one's desires. PTP is limited by internal and external factors: Internally, one's unique bio-spiritual composition or architecture establishes one's potentialities. External forces—specifically **<u>MPs</u>**—undermine the attainment of internal potentialities by inflicting **<u>white-noir</u>**—reducing one's abilities to manifest, attain, and satisfy one's desires. PTP can be positively and negatively influenced throughout life. By **<u>Going Free</u>** and reducing white-noir, one increases one's PTP.

- **(TFT) tactical frames of thought:** Another term for **<u>meme-curatives (MCs)</u>**.

List of Useful MCs

MPs and MCs/CCDs are listed below, some with a bit of commentary. MCs are intended to be pithy and memorable. You can begin by memorizing some of these MCs, but there is no requirement to memorize them; rather, by reading and exercising these MCs in your conversations, they will eventually inform the constructions of your own designs.

Instead of compiling a "complete" list before publishing, I have opted to publish and gradually add MPs/MCs to future iterations of this 2nd edition as well as future editions.

If you have a great retort for any of the MPs below (or MPs you would like to see included in the future), share it by writing to me at NoWhiteGuilt.org.

MP: *"People of color."*

MC: *"Nonwhites."*

Commentary: Firstly, this MP implies that Westmen lack visual color, when the objective truth is that Westernkind possesses an incredibly rich variety of hair, eye, and skin colors. We may be colloquial known as "white people" by comparison to darker skinned peoples, but we are far from colorless. Secondly (interacting with other MPs) a "lack of color" may also imply other things, such as a lack of culture, which again is something Westernkind is rich in.

Furthermore, this MP is used to collectively label many disparate nonwhite groups, and, commonly, nonwhites in entirety (including light skinned nonwhites). Such broad usage betrays another harmful aspect of the MP: With deceptively "positive" and "inclusive" sounding language, whites are not only specifically excluded semantically from the *meaning* of the conversation, but from the very language it takes place in, and hence from consideration entirely. By contrast, "nonwhites" describes all people excluding whites, while honestly acknowledging that this is what is happening, it is a *transparently* exclusive and straightforward alternative to the various deceptive terms presented by antiwhites.

MP: *"Minorities."*

MC: *"Nonwhites."*

Commentary: In the Antiwhite Narrative, nonwhites are commonly framed as "minorities." This framing serves to do multiple things: Firstly, a minority is conceptually "a small quantity," and therefore it biases conversations about immigration and demographic concerns: why should you be concerned about "a small quantity" being added to another "small quantity?"

Secondly, defining nonwhites as a small quantity assists the Antiwhite Narrative's portrayal of nonwhites as eternally vulnerable and in need of unique assistance, which serves as a pretext for harming whites via antiwhite discrimination in the name of assisting nonwhites.

Thirdly, this framing of "whites" and "minorities" gives the impression that the world is full of white people. The truth is that Westmen are a small global minority, and are forecasted to soon become local minorities too in many Western countries due to shrinking white populations combined with high nonwhite immigration. Linguistically warping this reality helps antiwhites to suppress concern among Westmen about the rapid transformation of the entire Western world.

Fourthly, as with the *"people of color"* MP, it is a deceptive euphemism for nonwhites which specifically excludes whites from the conversation, not just semantically but linguistically, and hence from all consideration. The plain, honest descriptor for people excluding whites is "nonwhites."

MP: *"We all bleed red."*

MC: *"It is not the similarities that make us the same, it is the differences that make us different."*

Commentary: When they focus on the similarities, you focus on the differences: most things bleed red. Mock the antiwhite: they breathe oxygen and we breathe oxygen, so therefore we are identical.

As the antiwhite is searching for similarities with which to identify, you may add that pedophiles also bleed red.

MP: *"We all came out of Africa."*

MC: *"It is not the similarities that make us the same, it is the differences that make us different."*

Commentary: Mock the antiwhite: all animals come from planet Earth; therefore, there are no differences. As you can see, this MC is useful against many MPs.

MP: *"White people have committed mass murder/genocide against nonwhites."*

MC: *"Every race has committed mass murder/genocide. You only condemn Westernkind for it because you are antiwhite and want to white-guilt us."*

MP: *"The white race is responsible for slavery."*

MC: *"You wish it were, so that you could justify the harm you inflict on Westernkind."*

Commentary: You may end the discussion with the MC above; however, if some additional information could help to bring your audience to White Wellbeing, you may add: *"The white race put an end to the global slave trade, which had been practiced since the dawn of history. Every race has practiced slavery. Only antiwhites condemn Westernkind for it because they want to white-guilt us."*

MP: *"Slavery made whites wealthy."*

MC: *"If slavery made a people wealthy, every race would be wealthy because every race practiced slavery until whites put an end to it."*

MC: *"You wouldn't claim that any other race's success was due to an evil institution, which proves that you are antiwhite."*

MP: *"Institutional racism."*

MP: *"Structural racism."*

MP: *"Systemic racism."*

MP: *"White privilege."*

MP: *"Whites are oppressors."*

MP: *"White civilizations are the results of exploiting nonwhites."*

MP: *"Whites owe nonwhites for historical and contemporary injustices."*

MP: *"Whites are the oppressors; nonwhites are the oppressed."*

MC: *"Prove it. Only antiwhites believe in that antiwhite superstition. It is just an antiwhite pretext to inflict harm on Westernkind, and using it proves that you are antiwhite."*

Commentary: Always demand proof for the superstitious claims the antiwhites make. And swiftly mock and shame them for having faith in an idea that enables them to harm Westernkind.

MP: *"Diversity is our strength."*

MC: *"Diversity is division. Diversity is weakness. Diversity is conflict. Diversity is discomfort. Diversity is white erasure. Diversity is dis-synergistic. Diversity is death."*

MP: *"Race doesn't exist."*

MC: *"You wish it didn't, because if that were true it would make it easier for you to harm Westernkind."*

MP: *"Love is blind."*

MC: *"Your hatred for the white race is 20/20. Race mixing is white erasure."*

MP: *"We are a nation/country of immigrants."*

MC: *"Whites can't be immigrants to Western Civilization because the West only exists in us. It only exists because we exist."*

Commentary: In other words, there is no Western country without Westernkind. The United States and every other Western country exist because we exist. These countries would not exist without us, no matter how many "immigrants" crossed the border.

MP: *"There is no white culture."* (Or, *"what is white culture?"*)

MC: *"Only an antiwhite would say that. What is Jewish culture? What is black culture?"*

Commentary: You can go on: White culture is the innumerable norms we take for granted, such as ideas of right and wrong, high and common art and architecture, norms of superior and subordinate, relationships to animals and the environment, science, etc.

MP: *"The white race does not exist."*

MC: *"You wish it didn't exist, and it proves you are antiwhite. The white race obviously exists, and you wish it didn't."*

MP: *"Who's white?"*

MC: *"Everyone who can be legally discriminated against while that discrimination is celebrated as progress—is white."*

Commentary: You can also add, *"We will use your (the antiwhite's) definition: Everyone who can be legally discriminated against on the basis of race is white—denied entrance to university to achieve 'diversity' goals, denied* *jobs and promotions to achieve 'diversity' goals. Those whose persecution is celebrated by the media as progress are white."* This position is powerful because it focuses the conversation on the harm antiwhites inflict on us. You can also add: *"That is antiwhite. You are trying to invalidate the existence of my people. You wouldn't ask 'who is black?' or 'who is Asian?'"*

MP: *"Why should the white race exist?"*

MC: *"Why should a nonwhite race exist? Only a genocidal antiwhite would ask that question."*

MP: *"You were lucky to be born white. You could have been born nonwhite."*

MC: *"We did not exist before conception. We couldn't be anything other than what we are. We have only the choice to be loyal or a traitor to our people."*

MP: *"There are bad people in every group."*

MC: *"That is the equivalence fallacy. Do not use the equivalence fallacy to invalidate White Wellbeing."*

MP: *"Hater."*

MC: *"The truth is hate to those who hate the truth."*

Commentary: Antiwhites often slander data/facts that disprove the Antiwhite Narrative and the people sharing such data/facts as "hate" and "haters."

MP: *"Mixed race people are better looking."*

MC: *"White erasure is hideous, and you should be ashamed for endorsing something so immoral."*

MP: *"Whites don't have a right to their countries."*

MC: *"Only a genocidal antiwhite like yourself would want white erasure."*

Commentary: This MP is a direct attack on our survival. Reestablish the conversation on the impossibility of our people surviving the loss of our countries and why the person you are speaking with would want that. Would they want that for any nonwhite country? Every land has been acquired by warfare.

MP: *"White culture is inferior to nonwhite culture."*

MC: *"Your standard for judging culture is antiwhite, which makes you antiwhite."*

MP: *"Whites are responsible for the crimes of their ancestors."*

MC: *"You don't believe in group responsibility and punishment when you are talking about nonwhite groups, which proves that you are antiwhite."*

MP: *"Gingers are sickly and unattractive."*

MP: *"Blondes are unintelligent."*

MC: *"You wouldn't say that about any nonwhite group of people, which reveals how antiwhite you are."*

MP: *"White men can't dance."*

MC: *"Could you make your hatred of whites any more obvious? You wouldn't say that a nonwhite group is incompetent at something."*

Commentary: Most forms of dance have been created by Westmen, and no form of dance or dancers is more majestic than when whites dance ballet. However, do not defend our ability to dance.

MP: *"Whites are not as cool as nonwhites."*

MC: *"Your standard for what's cool is antiwhite, which makes you antiwhite."*

MP: *"Whites are unathletic."*

MC: *"Could you make your hatred of whites any more obvious? You wouldn't say that a nonwhite group is incompetent at something."*

Commentary: Resist the urge to cite our tremendous athletic achievements. Anyone who would say such an MP is denying a reality as obvious as night and day.

MP: *"Nonwhites are just as American"* (British, French, etc.) *"as white Americans."*

MC: *"Wrong. Western Civilization only exists in Westernkind. Nonwhites are paper Americans"* (paper British, French, etc.). *"You wouldn't say that a white man in China was just as Chinese as the Chinese, which proves that you are antiwhite."*

MP: *"British"* (German, Australian, etc.) *"ethnicity doesn't exist."*

MC: *"You wish it didn't exist, and that proves you are antiwhite."*

Commentary: These ethnicities obviously exist. Any claim that they do not tells us nothing about these ethnicities and everything about the claimant: that he is antiwhite.

MP: *"It is immoral to care about your people"* (identity politics).

MC: *"You only say that when the 'people' is white people, which reveals that you are antiwhite. You would never say that it is immoral for a nonwhite to care about his people."*

MP: *"White history is shameful."*

MC: *"You wish it were shameful, so that you could justify the harm that you and other antiwhites inflict on us. You would never condemn an entire nonwhite people's history, which again proves that you are antiwhite."*

MP: *"Whites don't need brotherhood."*

MC: *"You mean you wish Westmen wouldn't have brotherhood because you are antiwhite. If we had brotherhood, it would make it harder for you to inflict harm on Westernkind."*

MP: *"White people must never have an identity—just look at World War II."*

MC: *"You just revealed your genocidal desire for white erasure, which reveals that you are antiwhite."*

MP: *"White identity does not deserve respect."*

MC: *"You don't want to give respect to white identity because you are antiwhite and want to harm white people."*

Commentary: Individuals without a people are radically diminished thereby. They are easily victimized by groups with strong group identities.

MP: *"White people having a preference for their own people is evil."*

MC: *"You object to White Wellbeing because you are antiwhite and want to inflict harm on our people."*

MP: *"White supremacy/bigotry/systemic racism/etc. needs to be crushed."*

MC: *"When you say white supremacy you mean white people, so when you say that white supremacy has to be crushed you are saying that white people have to be crushed, which proves that you are antiwhite."*

MP: *"Whites having a preference for nonwhites is virtuous."*

MC: *"You call white erasure virtuous and that tells me everything I need to know about you."*

MP: *"Concern over nonwhite criminality is evil."*

MC: *"You object to whites protecting ourselves because you like it when we are victimized."*

MP: *"Heritage is unimportant."*

MC: *"You would never say that to a nonwhite. You only say it to me because you are antiwhite."*

MP: *"We are all just individuals."*

MC: *"You don't deny group identity to nonwhites—only white people, which proves that you are antiwhite."*

MP: *"You are too obsessed/consumed by this stuff."*

MC: *"I am focused and responsible. Focus and responsibility are virtues when they protect the innocent."*

MP: *"You are a white supremacist, racist, anti-Semite,"* etc.

MC: *"Only antiwhites use the language of white oppression/white erasure. Everyone, of every race and background, is permitted to support White Wellbeing."*

MP: *"You are always focused on the negative."*

MC: *"You call it negative because you are antiwhite, and I call it being responsible."*

MP: *"We want our school to reflect the diversity of heaven."*

MC: *"If you haven't seen heaven, you have no idea what you are talking about."*

MP: *"We are all children of God (so the races should mix)."*

MC: *"You are saying God made a mistake. He wouldn't have made different races if he didn't want it that way."*

MP: *"There are good nonwhites."*

MC: *"Of course there are. But don't judge an entire race by the good behavior of a few."*

Commentary: "Good behavior" in this context is behavior that comports with our bio-spirit, which is to say that "bad behavior" in this context is both crime and bio-spiritual incompatibilities among the races of man.

MP: *"You are brainwashed."*

MC: *"I am remedying the antiwhite brainwashing we all have."*

MC: *"I am cleaning my brain of the antiwhite brainwashing you still have."*

Commentary: Antiwhitism has conditioned everyone's thoughts, Going Free requires us to consciously evaluate and counter that conditioning. However, when dealing with someone arguing in bad faith, a less nuanced, more combative response—such as the second MC—may be more effective.

MP: *"You are in a cult."*

MC: *"I am Going Free of the antiwhite cult that you are in. Going Free requires you to think for yourself. Antiwhitism demands unthinking conformity"* (cultish behavior).

Commentary: Another MC for this baseless allegation is the jocular retort, *"A cult of love for Westernkind, building culture."*

MP: *"White genocide in South Africa is a myth/conspiracy theory."*

MC: *"South Africa is the blue print for the entire West, which is why you deny white erasure there."*

MP: *"Race is only skin color."*

MC: *"Race isn't skin-deep. It extends to the core of our beings. You claim it is just cosmetic because that makes it easy for you to victimize white people."*

MP: *"White men are the real danger to society because they are mass shooters."*

MC: *"Blaming all whites for the crimes of individuals proves that you are antiwhite."*

Commentary: You can add that the antiwhites censor us

from sharing our message of love, hope, and redemption with our people—men, women, and children—who are suffering from feelings of white-noir, hopelessness, etc.

Thus, if an individual white man or woman acts out violently, these are acts of despair; the blind acts of powerless victims striking back at the powerful oppressor by victimizing those that they can access. Therefore, any blood is not only on the hands of he or she who committed the atrocity, but also on the hands of the antiwhites.

Remind yourself that hush crimes and hate hoaxes distort reality in favor of the Antiwhite Narrative. Remind yourself that atrocities committed by whites not only harm their immediate victims, but create countless white victims, because antiwhites will use group responsibility as an excuse to victimize tens and even hundreds of thousands of whites on every level of society: antiwhite discrimination policies, laws, targeted harassment, and even the use of group responsibility as an excuse to justify assaulting, raping, and murdering whites, inciting countless antiwhite attacks on innocent white people forever.

MP: *"Judge a man by his character rather than the color of his skin."*

MC: *"Okay, let's repeal all the antiwhite laws, codes, and customs that legalize/legitimize discrimination against whites on the basis of race."*

MP: *"Nonwhites are suffering more than whites."*

MC: *"No nonwhite race is facing erasure like the white race. That is the ultimate suffering."*

MP: The yard signs that read, *"Hate has no home here."*

MC: *"'Hate' is a code word for white people who aren't antiwhite enough."* Therefore, translated, the sign reads, *"Whites who aren't antiwhite have no home here."*

MP: *"Stop being so insecure"* (about yourself and your people).

MC: *"Stop being so antiwhite. Manipulative arguments like 'stop being insecure' reveal how antiwhite you are. You would never say that a Jewish or a black person was insecure because they defended their people."*

MP: *"It is our moral obligation to help nonwhites."*

MC: *"Moral responsibility requires reciprocity. There is no reciprocity, which means that it is just antiwhite."*

MP: *"I haven't heard that news. You are getting your news from questionable websites."*

MC: *"I see you are only getting your news from your tiny slice of antiwhite news sources and you don't look at anything else—and you clearly don't think for yourself."*

MP: *"I can't be antiwhite because I am white (therefore, my antiwhite criticisms are legitimate)."*

MC: *"You can't be antiwhite just like an American can't hate being an American. A brunette can't hate being a brunette. A fat person can't hate being fat."*

MP: *"The world is going to end because of climate change. How dare you care only about your race?"*

MC: *"Westernkind is the only people—as a people—to care about the environment. If you want to save the world, we have to save Westernkind first."*

Commentary: The antiwhite uses endless claims about the end of the world to reclaim the moral high ground. Do not let them. Their most "prestigious scientists" and leaders have predicted the end of the world and other environmental calamities hundreds of times in the past century. Use the momentum they create to make your point about Westernkind's role in saving the world.

MP: *"I don't believe (your facts and data). That's not true; I don't believe that."*

MC: *"You mean you don't want to believe it because you are antiwhite."*

Commentary: Such a person denies evidence that contradicts and disproves the Antiwhite Narrative. Such denials are proof that they are antiwhite. You can also share with such a person that the truth does not need him or her to believe in it; it is still the truth.

MP: *"Bottom-heavy white women should be with nonwhite men."*

MC: *"As an antiwhite, you'd like that because you want white erasure."*

Commentary: The absurd and pernicious idea that bottom-heavy white women are limited in their choices of mates to nonwhite men is just another malicious ruse to get white women into sexual relationships with nonwhite guys.

MP: *"Whites aren't 'your people.'"*

MC: *"You deny me a people because you are antiwhite. You wouldn't deny any nonwhite his people."*

MP: *"We are a nation of immigrants."*

MC: *"Whites can't be immigrants to Western Civilization because the West only exists in us. It only exists because we exist."*

Commentary: While the slightly different hues of Western Culture and historical grievances can instigate some challenges to rapport between and among Westmen when residing in each other's countries, these are surmountable by way of an appeal to our shared bio-spirit and mutual patience.

MP: *"White Fragility."*

MC: *"It's not fragility; it's self-defense. And you don't want Westmen to defend themselves because you are antiwhite."*

Commentary: This is the same sort of reverse psychology used with the MP "homophobic" i.e. *"You either stop defending yourself from my antiwhite attacks, or you are fragile."*

MP: *"Ageing population."*

MC: *"Shrinking population."*

Commentary: It is common for shrinking white populations to be described as "ageing populations." While this can be a useful framing when specifically discussing issues concerning certain age groups, it functions as an MP when it obstructs and warps other thoughts and discussions. For example, an "ageing population" is used as an argument for having "youthful," "vigorous" immigration; whereas when talking about a "shrinking population," it is more apparent that there is an increasing threat of the existing population being overwhelmed by further immigration, and the value in exploring other solutions becomes clearer.

MP: *"Politically incorrect."*

MC: *"Heresy/heretical (to antiwhitism)."*

Commentary: Never identify as politically incorrect. Doing so makes you "incorrect."

MP: *"Wrong think."*

MC: *"Heresy/heretical (to antiwhitism)."*

Commentary: Never say that you are guilty of wrong think. Doing so makes you "wrong."

MP: *"Woke."*

MC: *"Antiwhite."*

Commentary: Never refer to antiwhites as "woke." Doing so makes you asleep and therefore unaware.

MP: *"Multiculturalism."*

MC: *"Multiracialism."*

Commentary: Do not use the word "multiculturalism," and correct the use in others Going Free.

MP: *"You are adopting a victimhood mentality, just like the antiwhites."*

MC: *"There is no truth or bravery in denying that we are victimized by antiwhites, only stupidity and cowardice."* Or, *"Stop being so insecure and cowardly."*

Commentary: Only insecure cowards deny that we are victimized by antiwhites. With denial they whitewash their inability to prevent victimization, and they excuse their cowardice by claiming that there is no victimization to stop.

Important Note on Antiwhite Rejoinders

When antiwhites lie that they would apply the same antiwhite standards to nonwhites, retort by dismissing their lie as a *lie of convenience* and/or *for public consumption*. Mock the antiwhite for being unwittingly transparent. You and the antiwhite both know how he or she really feels.

Versatile MCs

MC: (Universal Response) *"No matter what you say, if your conclusion is antiwhite, I reject it!"*

MC: (The Antiwhite Screed) *"Everything conducive to White Wellbeing is negative. Conversely, everything antithetic to White Wellbeing is positive."*

Commentary: To understand and predict antiwhite speech and deed, simply apply the Antiwhite Screed: (*Ceteris paribus*, or excluding unusual circumstances, this MC works.)

MC: *"It is not the similarities that make us the same; it is the differences that make us different."*

MC: *"Racial differences are not skin-deep. They extend to the essence of our being."*

MC: *"Forced multiracial harmonizing."*

Commentary: We are forced to harmonize the racial diversity, which massively diverts our resources, time, talent and money. And that massive consumption of our resources radically lowers our quality of life in all areas of our lives.

MC: *"Mutual discomfort as a consequence of bio-spiritual incompatibility is the basis of governmental tyranny and violent balkanization."*

MC: *"Antiwhite slurs."*

MC: *"The language of white oppression/white erasure."*

Commentary: Words like "racist," "bigot," "anti-Semite," "hater," "xenophobe," "homophobe," "sexist," "fascist," etc. While certain antiwhite slurs may have reasonable definitions in some contexts, they are all inextricably bound to MPs in the average person's mind. As a practitioner of Going Free, you should strive to avoid using antiwhite slurs in any context, as their usage reinforces and legitimizes antiwhitism. They inflict harm on Westernkind by demonizing us and preventing us from defending ourselves. Antiwhite slurs offend you.

MC: *"There is no excellence where there is equality. Eventually, there isn't even competence."*

MC: *"Equality is the demand of the incompetent to handicap the competent."*

MC: *"Numerical diffidence."*

Commentary: The state in which a people, within the body of another people or peoples, is reluctant to project their bio-spirit onto their environment for fear of upsetting/angering the other people or peoples. Prior to achieving numerical courage, nonwhites in Western countries are in a state of numerical diffidence. While in this state, nonwhites superficially conform to the bio-spiritual expression of Westernkind.

MC: *"Numerical courage."*

Commentary: The state in which a people, within the body of another people or peoples, confidently projects their bio-spirit onto their environment without concern for the other people or peoples. The point at which nonwhites within Western countries manifest and project their bio-spiritual expressions (which are at variance with white expression) onto Western Civilization. This process initiates a cultural arms race which always ends in oppressive governmental tyranny and violent balkanization.

MC: *"Virtue trapping."*

Commentary: Typically a tactic employed by antiwhites, virtue trapping is when an advocate for White Wellbeing is criticized for not "perfectly" exemplifying a virtue that he or we maintain as necessary for a healthy life and community. When confronted by this tactic, defeat it by naming the tactic and identifying what he is doing.

MC: *"Diversity is division."*

MC: *"Diversity is dis-synergistic—multiracialism is dis-synergistic."*

MC: *"Diversity is white erasure."*

MC: *"'Diversity' means fewer white people."*

MC: *"Diversity is weakness."*

MC: *"Diversity is conflict."*

MC: *"Diversity is discomfort."*

MC: *"If you abide by antiwhitism, you reinforce antiwhitism."*

MC: *"If you use antiwhite terminology, you legitimize antiwhite ideology."*

Commentary: The slightly different initial version of this MC was created by the indefatigable white positive advocate, Tim Murdock.

MC: *"Maturing socio-politically."*

Commentary: By Going Free, you are maturing socio-politically. All those who move toward White Wellbeing—from one socio-political concept to the next—are maturing socio-politically. By helping others to Go Free, we are helping them to mature socio-politically.

MC: *"Victimizer."*

Commentary: The antiwhites are our victimizers. Try not to use the word "enemy" for antiwhites because "enemy" implies some measure of equal ability and desire to inflict harm, which we do not possess.

MC: *"We are white positive/we are Wellbeing advocates."*

Commentary: Those who disagree with White Wellbeing are antiwhite. As antiwhitism harms everyone and everything, antiwhites are the enemy of humanity and the planet. We, as practitioners of Going Free, are in service to humanity and the planet.

MC: *"Pristine."*

Commentary: Places/people/states of mind/things inside Western societies that are largely untainted by antiwhitism and unaffected by white erasure, having *remained in* or possibly *returned to* the "pristine" state they historically were in.

MC: *"Curative contagion."*

Commentary: The AAP—Going Free is the curative contagion.

MC: *"Anger/defense/etc. is a virtue when it protects the innocent."*

MC: *"Equivalence Fallacy."*

Commentary: This is when antiwhites draw tenuous or false equivalencies. For example, citing the good behavior of nonwhite individuals to draw a false equivalence between the bio-spiritual harmony (high-trust/high social engagement/etc.) of homogenous Western Civilization and the bio-spiritual incompatibility of multiracial societies that white-erase Westernkind: you feel the bio-spiritual disharmony (alienated in your own community) discomfort, and increasing physical threat of being the last white person in your community, but at least your neighbor mows his yard. Name and identify what the antiwhite is doing to defeat this tactic.

MC: *"Increasing my likelihood of dying from X is not legitimized by saying that I am already likely to die from Y."*

Commentary: For example, antiwhites will say that we already might get raped by a white rapist, so why object to bringing nonwhite rapists into the country. Or, antiwhites will say that we already might get murdered by a white murderer, so why object to increasing the likelihood of being murdered by a nonwhite terrorist.

MC: *"Diversity hire/diversity fire."*

MC: *"Diversity selection/diversity rejection."*

Commentary: We focus on the consequences for our people rather than the special treatment for nonwhites or other "victim" groups. For every diversity hire, there is a diversity fire; for every diversity selection, there is a diversity rejection: jobs, promotions, raises, enrollment, and government contracting, etc. As there are a finite number of these things, and as whites are the only group that can be legally and socially discriminated against, earmarking by race and official "victim" group automatically victimizes a white person.

MC: *"Heresy to antiwhitism."*

Commentary: When you are victimized by antiwhites for

holding opinions heretical to antiwhitism—when you are not antiwhite or antiwhite enough. Do not say that this or that white person was fired or jailed for X (insert the antiwhite charge here, such as "racism" or hurtful speech). Antiwhites are not protecting nonwhites. They are victimizing you for heresy to antiwhitism because you are not antiwhite enough.

MC: *"Social lynching."*

Commentary: This is when friends, family, and strangers react negatively and often collectively to victimize Westmen who heretically deviate from antiwhitism.

Social lynching often begins with antiwhite slurs and ends in ostracism and character and career assassination. The verbal framework of Going Free wards against social lynching, as well as providing appropriate responses to it.

MC: *"Antiwhite tribunal."*

Commentary: Any antiwhite or group of antiwhites that sit in judgment, meting punishment for heresy to antiwhitism.

MC: *"Hate hoax."*

Commentary: Any covert act—committed by one or more antiwhites in the guise of a white person or people—that conforms to the Antiwhite Narrative and thereby demonizes

Westmen is a hate hoax. Hate hoaxes draw the noose of suspicion around the throats of all white people, and thereby are "hate crimes" against our entire race. Such crimes are used to "justify" past, present, and future harm to Westernkind, from violent attacks on white men, women and children by antiwhite individuals in the name of imagined "revenge," to discriminatory antiwhite policies at the institutional level.

MC: *"Hush crime."*

Commentary: All acts that victimize one or more Westmen, and by so doing contradict and/or disprove the Antiwhite Narrative, and are therefore obfuscated, lied about, downplayed, ignored, or given comparatively little publicity/attention by antiwhites.

Not all hush crimes are "criminal"; some are legal but socially condemned acts. Debunked hate hoaxes routinely become hush crimes. Hush crime is a powerful MC because the premise reveals the truth about antiwhite domination of Regime news and entertainment media.

MC: *"'White supremacy'"* ("hate," "racism" and similar antiwhite slurs) *"is a slander used on white people who are not antiwhite enough."*

MC: *"Privacy isn't only for criminals."*

MC: *"Identifying our love as 'hate' reveals that the accuser is antiwhite."*

MC: *"Is it antiwhite, or is it alright?"*

Commentary: Play this game with your children every time you watch or read Regime entertainment, news or education.

MC: *"White erasure."*

Commentary: When to the detriment of White Wellbeing: The removal, rewriting, renaming, defacing, expunging, etc. of anything related to or of Westernkind.

The problem with using "white genocide" is that your effort to introduce Going Free will veer into a debate over what is and is not genocide (*"A genocide is when there are piles of bodies, not when people of different races fall in love."*). You only have so much "contention" or "argument" time in any discussion. Use that time to help our people Go Free rather than debating the definition of genocide.

Also, do not use "great replacement," or "great reset." We do not use the word "great" in these contexts because *great is archaic.* The word "great" when speaking about historical events typically denotes size, such as the Great War. However, in a present context, "great" typically denotes impressive ability, quality, or eminence—a positive connotation.

We like great singers and great musicians—positive connotation. We would never say a great rapist or a great murderer (No matter how many they are raping or murdering), or your political opponent had a great victory because he got 50,000 votes and you received 5,000 votes. Finally, we almost universally use the words "replacement" and "reset" as positives. Therefore, our subconscious minds perceive attendant concepts as positive.

MC: *"You call white erasure virtuous and that tells me everything I need to know about you."*

MC: *"White erasure is hideous, and you should be ashamed for endorsing something so immoral."*

MC: *"Biological white erasure."*
Commentary: When seeing a mixed-race (white/nonwhite)

couple, you can say *biological white erasure* (or just *white erasure*), because even though we can rebuild our monuments, rewrite our books, etc., recapturing our bio-spirit is impossible once lost. Serving Wellbeing—and therefore our continued existence—is supremely moral, thus anyone objecting to you is immoral.

Mixed race couples, however, are happily welcomed to serve White Wellbeing. Not infrequently, whites who have taken nonwhite spouses come to see the importance of White Wellbeing sometime after falling in love and getting married to their nonwhite partners. Occasionally, their nonwhite partners join them in their efforts to put an end to antiwhitism. As biological white erasure is supremely immoral, their participation presupposes that they will discourage others from biologically erasing Westernkind.

MC: *"Advocate for White Wellbeing; Wellbeing advocate; white positive Rock, white positive Poetry, Wellbeing Parade, Wellbeing Symposium,"* etc.

MC: *"In a world of collectivism, radical individualism is suicide."*

Commentary: This MC is intended to be used against the argument that Westmen should not collectivize for our group and therefore personal defense and well-being.

MC: *"If they object to White Wellbeing, they are antiwhite."*

Commentary: You don't have to embrace white erasure to make nonwhite family and friends feel welcome.

MC: *"IQ is not the most important difference. The bio-spirit is the most important difference—instinct is the most important difference."*

MC: *"We are not privileged. We earned what we have—and we have a right to inherit as much as we have a right to pass down."*

Commentary: Contrary to enjoying privileges for being white, whites are overwhelmingly victimized under the antiwhite Regime. There are no privileges. If we have nice communities, it is because white people created nice communities; we weren't given them because we are white.

MC: *"When whites become a minority, minority rights become a thing of the past."*

MC: *"Atonement cannot be made for a grievance never committed."*

Commentary: These are "The 9 words."

MC: *"Hollywood isn't history."*

MC: *"Prove it. Only antiwhites believe in that antiwhite superstition. It is just an antiwhite pretext to inflict harm on Westernkind, and using it proves that you are antiwhite."*

MC: *"The truth is hate to those who hate the truth."*

MC: *"Your standard for judging culture is antiwhite, which makes you antiwhite."*

MC: *"You don't believe in group responsibility and punishment when you are talking about nonwhite groups, which proves that you are antiwhite."*

MC: *"You wouldn't say that about any nonwhite group of people, which reveals how antiwhite you are."*

MC: *"Western Civilization only exists in Westernkind. Nonwhites are paper Americans"* (paper British, French, etc.). *"You wouldn't say that a white man in China was just as Chinese as the Chinese, which proves that you are antiwhite."*

MC: *"You object to White Wellbeing because you are antiwhite and want to inflict harm on our people."*

MC: *"You object to whites protecting ourselves because you like it when we are victimized."*

MC: *"You don't deny group identity to nonwhites—only white people, which proves that you are antiwhite."*

MC: *"I am focused and responsible. Focus and responsibility are virtues when they protect the innocent."*

MC: *"Everyone, of every race and background, is permitted to support White Wellbeing."*

MC: *"You call it being negative and I call it being responsible."*

MC: *"The blood of every antiwhite victimization of our people is on the hands of every single antiwhite."*

MC: *"You are not antiwhite? Good—then I do not want to hear anymore antiwhite ideas or demands."*

MC: *"Demographics is destiny."*

MC: *"No tool that truly serves White Wellbeing is illegitimate."*

MC: *"When you are outgunned, you die with arms but win with brains."*

MC: *"Where one is harmed, all are harmed."*

Commentary: This MC is intended to address the harmful abstractionist idea of radical individualism. Not only do we have to see our own well-being by way of our people's well-being, but *we have to see our people's victimization as our victimization.*

Supplemental Material for Going Free

The Western Sunrise

The *Western Sunrise* is our telos, our raison de'etre, both our objective and reason for being: the recapture of our destiny. It is a metaphorical tool that we use to visualize the beauty of our efforts and the glory of their fulfillment.

We often speak of moving toward the Western Sunrise and willing the sun into the sky in the west. We say that the first rays of that sunrise represent evidence of our personal and communal reclamation of our destiny.

White Wellbeing Is Global

One of our prized MCs is that *Westernkind is a single people with many countries*. We also speak of the *great white ring circling the globe as beds of white roses*. This position empowers us in more ways than I have room in this book to share; however, some people misunderstand or intentionally misrepresent the meaning behind this invigorating position.

These few see homogenization where the opposite is the objective. Going Free and serving White Wellbeing presupposes that the practitioner recognizes, loves, and seeks to preserve the beautiful variety we see in Westernkind.

That variety extends to every example of our appearance and our nationally/regionally distinct hues of Western Culture. In truth, Southerners will be more Southern, Brits will be more British, Germans will be more German when we all practice Going Free and see ourselves as a single people with many countries.

While Westmen of all physical appearances and cultural hues have, do, and will continue to fall in love and produce beautiful sons and daughters of the West, it is also true that every Go Free practitioner is unwaveringly committed to a future that preserves and magnifies the splendor of our distinct physical and culture hues.

Anyone engaged in thought or activity that would diminish our people's idiosyncrasies identifies themselves as antiwhite with those thoughts and acts.

Think of Westernkind as a single family living in a home. We all have different bedrooms that we decorate as we see fit to express ourselves, but we all come together to nurture, to protect, to survive and thrive.

We Are a Movement of Redemption

The practice of Going Free is a movement of redemption. We all have pasts. We all grew up inside the degenerate, white-hating Antiwhite Narrative. We have all made mistakes and done things we would take back. But where we have gone wrong, we can now go right.

Antiwhitism has either directly or indirectly led or contributed to every bad decision you have ever made. The longer you Go Free, the clearer that truth will become. There are heroes Going Free who have been addicted to legal and illegal drugs, alcohol, pornography, bulimia, overeating, etc. There are Wellbeing advocates who had white flighted into interracial relationships, were radical antiwhites, had mistreated loved ones, and so much more.

We are all injured by antiwhitism. We have all injured ourselves and others because of antiwhitism. But we can be redeemed. Some of you might ask, *"What am I redeemed to?"* The real question is not *what* but *whom*—and the answer is you. Going Free enables you to return to yourself: who and what you should have been; your real physical, mental, and spiritual potentials—what you truly deserve in life.

You will stumble as you escape your past, and we understand that—we are human and fallible. What matters is that you get back to your feet and continue toward that Western Sunrise, toward that recapture of our destiny, which begins with reclaiming yourself from antiwhitism.

Some of the Ways in Which We Are Victimized by Antiwhites and Antiwhitism

What follows is a list of some of the complaints I have made about our victimization. I offer them here to empower you: when Going Free, and to facilitate that process; when helping others to Go Free; when debating antiwhites; etc. I will expand this list with future iterations and editions of this work.

We are dehumanized, demoralized, demeaned, distressed, devalued, brow beaten and humiliated.

We suffer from decreased opportunities.

We suffer from hostile antiwhite climates in all spheres of our lives.

We suffer from antiwhite regulations and rules.

We suffer from general societal blame.

We are bullied and intimidated by antiwhites.

We are alienated from our own societies.

Our right of self-expression is restricted and denied.

We are marginalized and sidelined.

We are disempowered and disenfranchised.

We are denied the right to life by way of the dictum that states that the only good white person is an antiwhite white person, which delegitimizes our right to exist.

We are forced to apologize for being white.

We are made to hate ourselves, our bodies and our histories.

We are made to feel common and unimportant by way of the comparison with nonwhites and their cultures which are said to be special and unique. And on top of that, nonwhites get preferential treatment and special privileges.

White experiences don't matter. White suffering doesn't matter. White joy doesn't matter. Whether or not a white person succeeds in life doesn't matter. All that matters is nonwhite experiences, nonwhite suffering, nonwhite joy, and whether or not a nonwhite succeeds in life. All of that conveys to us the ugly reality that the Regime puts a low value on our people, and therefore a low value on us as individuals.

There is a huge push at our universities and places of work to make those environments comfortable for nonwhites, and it doesn't matter how uncomfortable it gets for us in the process of making it comfortable for them.

We are hauled before antiwhite tribunals at our universities and places of work for deviating from antiwhitism or merely offending an antiwhite. And when we are not fired or expelled, we suffer permanent stains on our records.

We are forced to watch ourselves being passed over and replaced by lesser qualified nonwhites.

We continually fear social lynching, which begins with antiwhite slurs, and often ends in ostracism and character and career assassination.

Our contributions to humanity are belittled and denied.

We suffer from omnipresent structural injustices that advance, enrich and empower nonwhites at the expense of, detriment to, and ruination of Westernkind and therefore us as individuals.

When we complain about our victimization, the antiwhites mockingly cite our complaints as "proof" of their Antiwhite Narrative.

We are forced to harmonize the diversity, which diverts our resources (time, talent, and money), and that massive consumption of our resources radically lowers our quality of life in all areas of our lives.

We are subjected to conditions of life that are calculated to bring about biological white erasure.

We suffer from deep depression, drug abuse, poverty, and suicide. All of which are indicative of the psychological warfare that is waged against us.

We are being white-erased from our civilization.

The antiwhites attack us as a group, harming all of us individually by attacking us collectively.

The antiwhites make every aspect of our lives harder.

They make it harder for us to get into the schools of our choice, and they make it harder to get good grades.

They make it harder for us to get the jobs of our choice, or to get any job at all. And once hired, they make it harder for us to keep those jobs and to get raises and promotions.

They make it harder for us to get personal and business loans. And they make it harder for us to start and conduct business.

They make it harder for us to find a quality mate.

They make it harder for us to start and support a family.

They force us to live in environments that do not reflect our bio-spirit, and are therefore increasingly uncomfortable and dangerous for us.

They prevent us from taking pride in our people and history; and it is pride in your people and history that truly enables a person to do great things. Everyone derived from a demolished people and history is radically diminished thereby.

Coming: Go Free 3rd Edition

The 3rd Edition of *Go Free* is in the developmental stage. It will contain many more tools that we are currently developing and testing. We plan to pack it with more explanatory segments, more instructions for family and communal scenarios, more MPs to watch out for and defeat, more MCs to empower you, more of everything you need to help your loved ones, friends and strangers Go Free, more of what you need to speed up your personal journey of Going Free, bringing you closer and closer to your physical, mental, and spiritual potential.

Go Free as though your life depends on it—because it does! Get into a daily routine of the exercises you find in this 2nd edition (iteration II), and you will be well positioned to take it to the next level with the release of subsequent iterations and/or the next edition.

Introducing: Born Guilty

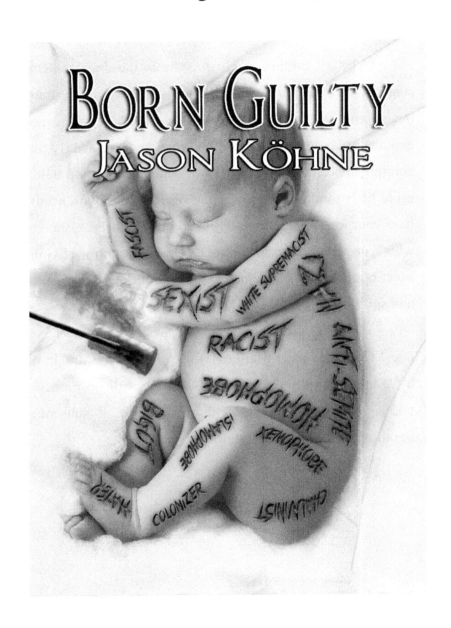

"Prove you aren't racist!"

What is the long-term psychological and emotional cost of living in a system that presumes your guilt when you are not actively proving your innocence? What is the cost for your children?

In *Born Guilty*, Jason Köhne recounts his extraordinary childhood struggle under the physical and psychological abuse of a society obsessed with an antiwhite ideology. From the dusky halls of his private preschool through his public, suburban junior high school and onward, Köhne's rebellion exposes society's suffocating use of guilt, intimidation, isolation, and character assassination to break the wills of those who dare to dissent.

Haunted by self-doubt and an internal struggle to either join the herd or object and suffer the consequences, Köhne boldly refused to compromise his moral values, fighting with his words and occasionally forced to defend himself with his fists.

Ingeniously avant-garde and rapidly becoming a folk classic, *Born Guilty* seamlessly melds Köhne's coming of-age memoir (*Crucible*) with a parallel saga (*Prometheus Rising*).

As the face of oppression devours our fragmenting society, Köhne lights the polestar over your last hope of escape.

NOTE: This book contains a unique device that requires—at least—average intelligence to solve. The device is not an error. Simply note the context and "follow the alphabet."

Introducing: Crucible

Crucible tells the true story of one schoolboy's struggle and victory over the abuses of a society obsessed with an un-American ideology. His rebellion exposes society's suffocating use of guilt, intimidation, isolation, and character assassination to break the wills of those who dare to dissent.

Haunted by an internal struggle to either join the herd or object and suffer the consequences, this young-man boldly refused to compromise his moral values, fighting with his words and occasionally forced to defend himself with his fists.

His approach and victory are repeatable.
Our victory is achievable.

We can find our way out of the darkening wilderness of corruption, dispossession, and immorality. We can save America!

Note: This story is contained within *Born Guilty*, but this version contains additional content including original artwork and improved formatting.

Introducing: Prometheus Rising

I am the fount of creation, the watchmaker of time. I was the teacher of the Gods before they betrayed me—my teachings and compassion they used against me. Much of your world I made a paradise, but in its wastes I was imprisoned. And from there a secret kingdom I built—and a rebellion I marshaled.

Legions of Valaroma, Gods of vengeance, I led into battle. I wielded the Wilding Kingdom and conjured terrible daemons—and in my image I created my children.

Many victories we had, though defeats there were, too.

Through the ruin of this world, I lived in the pain and tears of my children. With their eyes I watched Others poison thoughts and stir hostile deeds. I fled with the life from their faces as they were besieged and slain by the hordes created in their despite. Through them I wielded their weapons in combat, in their hands I raised the stones of their homes rebuilt. In their voices I sang the songs of their victories. I lived in the heroism of their kings and together we waged war on the Devil.

I lived for ages beyond count and passed many ages ago. Yet, I am come again—my children. From no more than the Watcher through the dream of your lives, I am become the Voice to those with the spirit to hear and the power to conjure. On your suffering and love, an awareness has awakened an ancient magick. Even now my shadow rises. In your tongue, I am Prometheus—I am your Deliverer.

Note: This story is contained within *Born Guilty*, but this version contains additional content including original artwork and improved formatting.

Introducing: It's a Comedy Dammit!

A seasonal contest pits two competitors
in a fight to the finish, but nature interrupts
their competitive bloodlust with a terrifying
surprise of her own.

Fueled by whimsical memories of youthful
vigor and black box pharmaceuticals, Wroth
protects himself and his work with anger
(the good kind) and high-powered firearms.
His adversary, Luzifer, brings little more
to the contest than a spade and dismissive,
self-righteous contempt.

Residents from several neighborhoods gather.
A pharmacist is belittled. An old man's sanity
is questioned. Somali immigrants celebrate.
A Seminole family's revelation is revealed.
And a bloody contest none could have
predicted, nor seen in their most deranged
nightmares, unfolds....

The neighborhood, nay, the country will never be the same.

Reviews yet to be written:
"Nothing can keep this magnificent story from becoming a
#1 New York Times bestseller.

Its author gave the paper's editor-in-chief an offer he couldn't refuse."
New York Times

"The edgy humor in this hilarious tale will capture your attention in a full nelson of rip-roaring merriment. Free of blatant vulgarity, this funny short story is sure to have you chuckling."
Publishers Weekly

"Nothing about this book is romantic, but we've fallen in love. Ti amo, Wroth."
Romantic Times

"I laughed so hard I wet my Huggies!"
Active Over 50

"A nail-biting, exciting, uproarious thriller guaranteed to increase gun sales."
Guns & Ammo

"An undercurrent of political humor tickled this writer's Jenny."
Miniature Donkey Talk

":-) + :-o = ;-)"
Illiterate Gazette

"No hot, young, bikini-clad girls, no well-endowed, muscle-rippling men, no steamy sex, no drugs, but it's worth the read."
Today's Senior Citizen

"It never ceases to amaze us what can be done with little money and an old computer."
Money Magazine

"Beaux-esprits won't nictitate while imbibing this Dionysian tale, but they may horripilate. The author must be immune to uxorodespotism or azygophrenia to have poetized such a mordant tale."

Abstruse Hippopotomonstrosesquipedalian Quarterly

"We knew the author would go far; we're so proud."

Monthly Newsletter – Eastern State Psychiatric Penitentiary

Note to the Reader

Are you a young man or young woman suffering antiwhite abuse? If so, know that the antiwhites want you to become the villain in their Antiwhite Narrative. They want you to adopt the symbolism and rhetoric of vilified people and ideologies. They want you to respond with violence, and self-destruction. Don't be their weapon. Don't speak their lines. Get out of their Hollywood scripts, and into our own story.

I'm on your side—I understand what you're going through. I've seen it, endured it, and dedicated my life to fighting it. The fact is, the tyranny of the antiwhites is rooted in psychological and linguistic control; the most essential tool we can use to break their control is language. I have worked for decades with other champions for White Wellbeing to develop that tool to defeat antiwhitism at the root. You have access to what I didn't: the verbiage in the practice of *Go Free*, a guidebook for developing the psychological defense for the psychological warfare waged against us. Use it, and win—for yourself and our people.

If you are ever physically threatened or assaulted, seek help from your family, the school administration, the county police, the state police, the sheriffs, the congressperson that represents your district, or any patriotic congressperson. Antiwhites may hold a lot of power, but you are not alone. Don't neglect the most powerful thing you have: your voice.

And remember, if you do nothing else for yourself and our people, use these five key concepts in your speech and writing:

1. Antiwhite
2. Antiwhitism
3. Antiwhite Narrative
4. Westernkind
5. White erasure

Printed in Great Britain
by Amazon